SHEPHERD'S NOTES

SHEPHERD'S NOTES

When you need a guide through the Scriptures

Ezekiel

BROADMAN
& HOLMAN
PUBLISHERS

Nashville, Tennessee

0–8054–9078–7
Dewey Decimal Classification: 224.40
Subject Heading: BIBLE. O.T. EZEKIEL
Library of Congress Card Catalog Number: 97–45161

Library of Congress Cataloging-in-Publication Data
Ezekiel / Paul P. Enns, editor
    p. cm. — (Shepherd's notes)
Includes bibliographical references.
ISBN 0–8054–9078–7
1. Bible. O.T. Ezekiel—Study and teaching.
I. Lintzenich, Robert. II. Series
BS1315.5.R88   1998
224'.407—dc21
                                    97–45161
                                         CIP

CONTENTS

Foreword vi

How to Use This Book vii

Introduction 1

The Prophet's Call (1:1–3:27) 6

Prophecies against Judah and
Jerusalem (4:1–24:27) 11

Judgment against the Nations
(25:1–32:32) 61

Prophecies of Israel's Restoration
and Blessing (33:1–39:29) 79

Prophecies of Worship in the
Millennial Kingdom (40:1–48:35) 95

Bibliography 101

Dear Reader:

Shepherd's Notes are designed to give you a quick, step-by-step over-view of every book of the Bible. They are not meant to be substitutes for the biblical text; rather, they are study guides intended to help you explore the wisdom of Scripture in personal or group study and to apply that wisdom successfully in your own life.

Shepherd's Notes guide you through the main themes of each book of the Bible and illuminate fascinating details through appropriate com-mentary and reference notes. Historical and cultural background information brings the Bible into sharper focus.

Six different icons, used throughout the series, call your attention to historical-cultural information, Old Testament and New Testament references, word pictures, unit summaries, and personal application for everyday life.

Whether you are a novice or a veteran at Bible study, I believe you will find *Shepherd's Notes* a resource that will take you to a new level in your mining and applying the riches of Scripture.

In Him,

David R. Shepherd
Editor-in-Chief

HOW TO USE THIS BOOK

DESIGNED FOR THE BUSY USER

Shepherd's Notes for Ezekiel is designed to provide an easy-to-use tool for getting a quick handle on this Bible book's important features, and for gaining an understanding of its message. Information available in more difficult-to-use reference works has been incorporated into the *Shepherd's Notes* format. This brings you the benefits of many advanced and expensive works packed into one small volume.

Shepherd's Notes are for laymen, pastors, teachers, small-group leaders and participants, as well as the classroom student. Enrich your personal study or quiet time. Shorten your class or small-group preparation time as you gain valuable insights into the truths of God's Word that you can pass along to your students or group members.

DESIGNED FOR QUICK ACCESS

Bible students with time constraints will especially appreciate the time-saving features built into the *Shepherd's Notes*. All features are intended to aid a quick and concise encounter with the heart of the message.

Concise Commentary. Ezekiel is one of the major prophetic books of the Bible and perhaps one of the most neglected. Ezekiel combines three forms of literature—narrative, prophetic addresses, and apocalyptic. The latter form of literature is characterized by highly symbolic language and imagery which is difficult to interpret and easy to misinterpret. These elements in Ezekiel may be one of the reasons this prophecy is studied as little as it is. And yet, Ezekiel is a portion of God's written Word. It was a powerful message to God's people in exile six centuries before Christ. For us today it points to enduring spiritual truths that we do well to understand and build our lives on.

Outlined Text. A comprehensive outline covers the entire text of Ezekiel. This is a valuable feature for following the flow of the book, allowing for a quick, easy way to locate a particular passage.

Shepherd's Notes. These summary statements appear at the close of every key section of the narrative. While functioning in part as a quick summary, they also deliver the essence of the message presented in the sections which they cover.

Icons. Various icons in the margin highlight recurring themes in Ezekiel and aid in selective searching or tracing of those themes.

Sidebars and Charts. These specially selected features provide additional background information to your study or preparation. These include definitions as well as cultural, historical, and biblical insights.

Maps. These are placed at appropriate places in the book to aid your understanding and study of a text or passage.

Questions to Guide Your Study. These thought-provoking questions and discussion starters are designed to encourage interaction with the truth and principles of God's Word.

DESIGNED TO WORK FOR YOU

Personal Study. Using the *Shepherd's Notes* with a passage of Scripture can enlighten your study and take it to a new level. At your fingertips is information that would require searching several volumes to find. In addition, many points of application occur throughout the volume, contributing to personal growth.

Teaching. Outlines frame the text of Ezekiel, providing a logical presentation of the message. Capsule thoughts desginated as "Shepherd's Notes" provide summary statements for presenting the essence of key points and events. Application icons point out personal application of this message, and Historical Context icons indicate where background information is supplied.

Group Study. *Shepherd's Notes* can be an excellent companion volume to use for gaining a quick but accurate understanding of the message of a Bible book. Each group member can benefit by having his or her own copy. The *Note's* format accommodates the study of or the tracing of the major themes in Ezekiel. Leaders may use its flexible features to prepare for group sessions or use them during group sessions. Questions to guide your study can spark discussion of Ezekiel's key points and truths.

LIST OF MARGIN ICONS USED IN EZEKIEL

 Shepherd's Notes. Placed at the end of each section, a capsule statement that provides the reader with the essence of the message of that section.

 Old Testament Reference. Used when the writer refers to Old Testament Scripture passages that are related or have a bearing on the passage's understanding or interpretation.

 New Testament Reference. Used when the writer refers to New Testament passages that are related to or have a bearing on the passage's understanding or interpretation.

 Historical Background. To indicate historical, cultural, geographical, or biographical information that sheds light on the understanding or interpretation of a passage.

 Personal Application. Used when the text provides a personal or universal application of truth.

 Word Picture. Indicates that the meaning of a specific word or phrase is illustrated so as to shed light on it.

TITLE

The title of the book is taken from its author and main character. It is mentioned only twice in the book (1:3; 24:24) .

AUTHORSHIP

Internally, the book gives evidence that Ezekiel wrote the book that bears his name. He wrote in the first person (1:1; 8:1; 20:1; 24:1) which also indicates the unity of the book, not multiple authorship. The chronology of the book also suggests a structural unity (1:2; 8:1; 20:1; 24:1; 29:1; 31:1; 32:1; 40:1). The book unfolds both logically and chronologically from 593 B.C. to 573 B.C., indicating an inherent unity.

Ezekiel's name means "God strengthens."

Finally, the book itself gives evidence of structural unity: Ezekiel's call (chaps. 1–3), prophecies of judgment against Judah and Jerusalem (chaps. 4–24), prophecies of judgment against other nations (chaps. 25–32), prophecies of restoration and blessing (chaps. 33–39), and worship in the millennium (chaps. 40–48). This pattern follows the normal pattern of prophetic writings:

- judgment of Judah or Israel;
- judgment of the nations; and
- the hope of future restoration and blessing.

DATE

Ezekiel was taken captive into Babylon in 597 B.C. in the fifth year of King Jehoiachin's exile and began his ministry in 593 B.C. (1:2). This is further supported in the statement "the twelfth year of our exile" in 33:21. Since Jerusalem fell in

586 B.C., Ezekiel's captivity would have taken place in 597 B.C.

The prophecies unfold in orderly fashion:

CHAPTERS	PROPHECY	DATES
1–24	Predicts Jerusalem's fall	593–588 B.C.
25–33	God's judgment against the nations (except 29:17–21)	587–585 B.C.
33–48	Israel's future restoration and blessing in the millennial kingdom	585–573 B.C.

The chronology of the book is evident in 1:1–2; 8:1; 20:1; 24:1; 26:1; 29:1, 17; 30:20; 31:1; 32:1, 17; 33:21; 40:1. Ezekiel probably wrote the book within the time period of the events, likely 593–570 B.C.

EZEKIEL THE MAN

Not only was Ezekiel one of the major prophets; he was also a priest (7:26; 22:26), particularly evident in the millennial section (chaps. 40–48).

Facing a people who thought the captivity would soon end and they would return to the land of Israel, Ezekiel warned the Israelites in exile that they would not soon return; instead, Jerusalem would be judged and destroyed because of the rampant idolatry of the people (chaps. 4–24). In chapters 33–48 Ezekiel provided hope and encouragement to the captives, detailing Israel's future restoration and blessing in the millennial kingdom.

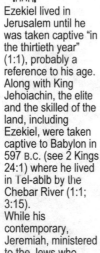

Ezekiel lived in Jerusalem until he was taken captive "in the thirtieth year" (1:1), probably a reference to his age. Along with King Jehoiachin, the elite and the skilled of the land, including Ezekiel, were taken captive to Babylon in 597 B.C. (see 2 Kings 24:1) where he lived in Tel-ablb by the Chebar River (1:1; 3:15). While his contemporary, Jeremiah, ministered to the Jews who remained in the land, Ezekiel ministered to the complacent Jews in exile in Babylon, ministering for approximately 20 years, from 593 B.C. onward (see 1:1; 40:1).

Ezekiel ministered in unusual ways, using symbolic acts to communicate his prophetic messages. For example, he built a city and laid siege to it (4:1–3); he lay on his side, illustrating the captivity of the Northern and Southern Kingdoms (4:4–8); he ate defiled bread with limited water supply (4:9–17); he shaved his head (5:1–17). Ezekiel was also relatively silent until Jerusalem was captured (3:26–27; 24:27; 29:21) apart from specific occasions when the elders came to speak to him (8:1; 20:1). After that time, Ezekiel spoke freely (33:22).

HISTORICAL BACKGROUND

Following Solomon's death in 931 B.C., the nation of Israel divided into two nations, the Northern Kingdom (Israel) and the Southern Kingdom (Judah). The Northern Kingdom continued in apostasy throughout its history and was finally destroyed and the people taken captive into Assyria in 722 B.C. Later, in 701 B.C., the Assyrian king Sennacherib extended his military tentacles into the south, destroying 46 towns and villages in Judah in 701 B.C. (2 Kings 18:13ff.). In 612 B.C. the Babylonians destroyed Nineveh and the Assyrian empire and established themselves as the supreme power, consolidating its power by defeating Pharaoh Neco at Carchemish in 605 B.C. Pharaoh Neco had placed Jehoiakim on the throne of Judah as his vassal (2 Kings 23:31–35).

Having defeated Pharaoh Neco, Nebuchadnezzar, king of Babylon, invaded Judah in 605 B.C. and launched the first captivity and deportation to Babylon—which included Daniel (Dan. 1:1–7). When Jehoiachin, Jehoiakim's son, assumed the throne, Nebuchadnezzar invaded a second time and took ten thousand officers, craftsmen, and artisans captive, including

"Israel"

While originally the term *Israel* designated the entire nation of twelve tribes, after the division of the kingdom in 931 B.C., "Israel" referred to the ten northern tribes while "Judah" referred to the Southern Kingdom. In 722 B.C. the Northern Kingdom went into captivity and only Judah remained. Ezekiel dealt with the Southern Kingdom; however, the term *Israel* is used throughout the book of Ezekiel both as a synonym for Judah and also to designate the entire nation.

Ezekiel (2 Kings 24:8–17). Only the poor remained in Judah (2 Kings 24:14). Nebuchadnezzar installed Zedekiah, a weak king, as his puppet on the throne of Judah. But Zedekiah, encouraged by a pro-Egyptian faction, rebelled against Babylon (2 Kings 24:20; Jer. 27:1–11), eliciting Nebuchadnezzar's third invasion of Jerusalem. Following a two-year siege, in 586 B.C., Jerusalem was captured, pillaged, and burned. Zedekiah was blinded, his sons killed, and he was taken in chains to Babylon (2 Kings 25:1–12).

The destruction of Jerusalem was a solemn reminder to the Jews in captivity in Babylon that their stay in Babylon would not be short. As a result, the Jews settled down in Babylon, built houses, raised crops, and became successful merchants (Jer. 29:5; Ezra 2:68–69). In 539 B.C. the Medo-Persians conquered the Babylonians. King Cyrus of Persia issued the decree permitting the Jews to return to their homeland and rebuild the Temple (Ezra 1:1–4).

PURPOSE OF THE BOOK
The Old Testament prophets commonly had a twofold message: judgment for sin and future restoration and blessing in Messiah's kingdom. The book of Ezekiel follows this pattern. Chapters 4–32 detail the messages of judgment against Judah and the nations. In chapter 8 Ezekiel detailed the idolatry of the elders, women, and priests—their sinfulness necessitating the departure of the glory of God (11:23). The false prophets (chap. 13) and elders (chap. 14) were responsible for the idolatry and moral collapse. Judah's faithlessness is illustrated in the parable of the faithless wife (chap. 16). The sins of Judah culminated in the death of Ezekiel's wife, illustrating the death of the nation (24:24).

But the prophet also provided hope: Chapters 33–48 describe Israel's future restoration and worship in Messiah's kingdom. Israel will be regenerated spiritually (36:25–27), and the reunited nation will be restored to the land (chaps. 36–37), culminating in the establishment of the millennial temple (chaps. 40–48).

QUESTIONS TO GUIDE YOUR STUDY

1. What does the name *Ezekiel* mean?
2. What are the dates of Ezekiel's prophecies?
3. With what key event in Israel's history was Ezekiel associated ?
4. What was the twofold message of most prophets in the Old Testament?

Ezekiel's vision was similar to Isaiah's (Isa. 6) and that of the apostle John (Rev. 4–5).

Ezekiel wrote from Babylon, where the Hebrew people had been taken captive by King Nebuchadnezzar. Because of Israel's disobedience and apostasy, God sent Nebuchadnezzar as His "rod of chastisement" against Israel; the foreign king invaded Israel three times—in 605, 597, and 586 B.C.—finally burning and destroying Jerusalem. Ezekiel was taken captive in 597 B.C.

THE PROPHET'S CALL (1:1–3:27)

INTRODUCTION (1:1–3)

Ezekiel 1 is one of the most unusual chapters in Scripture—but there is a reason for it. Ezekiel ministered to an apostate nation. For the prophet to fully understand the depravity of Israel, it was essential that he have a proper understanding of the holiness of God. Chapter 1 details Ezekiel's vision of the exalted, righteous Lord. With that understanding, Ezekiel would have a true perspective of his ministry to an unrighteous nation.

Ezekiel was thirty years old—the age when Israelite men began to serve as priests (Num. 4:23, 30, 39, 43)—when he had a vision of God in 597 B.C. (1:1). King Jehoiachin, the disobedient king of Israel, had been captured by Babylon in 597 B.C. Amid this disobedience in the nation, Ezekiel received a vision from God in which the Lord revealed Himself to the prophet and gave him a message to the people.

EZEKIEL'S VISION (1:4–28)

The Four Living Creatures (1:4–14)

In the storm, wind, cloud, and fire, God revealed His presence, recalling His presence on Mount Sinai (Exod. 19:16) and His revelation to Elijah (1 Kings 19:11–12). What did all this represent? It was a manifestation of the glory of God (1:28), designed to inspire awe and reverence for His name.

The four living creatures that appeared to Ezekiel are identified as cherubim (vv. 5–10; cp. 10:18). The burning coals of fire coming from the midst of the cherubim anticipated the judgment upon Jerusalem in 586 B.C. that was inflicted by Nebuchadnezzar (2 Kings 25:9).

The Four Wheels (1:15–21)

Beneath the cherubim were wheels that sparkled like beryl, a precious, gold-colored stone. The wheels were at right angles to each other, rolling in all four directions, indicating God could (and would) move to judge, in whatever direction necessary. The wheels had eyes (v. 18), suggesting God's omniscience—God saw the nation in its sin and apostasy—and He was moving to judge.

The Expanse (1:22–25)

Above the cherubim was an expanse like crystal that sparkled like ice. This was like a platform on which God's throne rested. The brilliance of the precious stones (vv. 16, 22, 26) revealed the brilliant shekinah glory of God (cp. Rev. 4:6). The sound of the cherubim flying was awesome, designed to bring reverence and worship to an infinitely holy God (v. 24).

The Throne (1:26–28)

Above the expanse was the throne of God, made of costly sapphire (Job 28:16; cp. Exod. 24:10). John described this as a foundation stone in the New Jerusalem (Rev. 21:19). On the throne Ezekiel saw the representation of a man, a theophany (cp. Dan. 7:13). It was a manifestation of God but not the essence of God, for no person can see God's essence and live (Exod. 33:20; John 1:18).

In the Old Testament, God revealed Himself in a variety of ways: visions (Ezek. 1), dreams (Dan. 2), theophanies (Gen. 18), audible spoken word (Exod. 19). With the coming of Jesus Christ, God has revealed Himself in a superior way—through His Son—and that message is accurately recorded in His written Word (Heb. 1:1–2).

Cherubim are guardians of the holiness of God (Rev. 4:6–9). They were present at the expulsion of Adam and Eve from the Garden of Eden (Gen. 3:24); the cherubim rested above the ark of the covenant (Exod. 25:18–20). They were also embroidered in the curtain of the tabernacle (Exod. 26:1; 36:8). They are distinguished from seraphim (Isa. 6:2).

The foundation for an effective ministry is understanding who God is. If we have a concept of the awesome holiness of God, we will see ourselves and others in a true light—as sinful people—and this will have a profound effect on our ministry.

God addressed Ezekiel as "son of man" (2:1). The term is used ninety-three times in Ezekiel, and it emphasizes the frailty and true humanity of the prophet (cp. Ps. 8:4). When applied to Christ, it took on a unique meaning. As Son of Man, Christ was the promised Messiah, designed to establish God's kingdom on earth (Dan. 7:13). In the New Testament, this term is basically a synonym for "Son of God" (see John 5:25, 27).

■ *It was essential for Ezekiel to have a picture*
■ *of God's awesome greatness before he could*
■ *minister and confront an apostate people*
■ *with their sin.*

EZEKIEL'S COMMISSION (2:1–3:3)

To an Unfaithful People (2:1–4)

Following Ezekiel's vision of the exalted Lord, the prophet received his commission to the exiled people of Judah in Babylon. Ezekiel's vision and commissioning paralleled that of Isaiah (Isa. 6:6–13).

Ezekiel's commission was not easy: He was sent to the exiles of Judah, a "rebellious people" (v. 3), and a "stubborn and obstinate" people (v. 4).

With a Faithful Message (2:5–3:3)

In spite of the obstinacy of the people, the Lord commanded Ezekiel to be fearless and faithful in delivering the message. The thistles, thorns, and briars represent the hostility and hardness of the Israelites—but Ezekiel was to be courageous. What was his responsibility? "Speak my words . . . "(v. 7). The Lord commanded Ezekiel, "Open your mouth and eat . . . a scroll."

The prophet was to warn the exiles that the Babylonians would destroy Jerusalem. God fed Ezekiel the scroll (3:2), meaning Ezekiel received the message from the Lord both in knowledge and by personal conviction. The prophet found the message "sweet as honey"—although Ezekiel was called on to pronounce a message of judgment, it was just and appropriate.

N

- *God sent Ezekiel with a message of judgment*
- *to the rebellious Israelites in exile in Baby-*
- *lon. They would be stubborn and resistant;*
- *yet he was to be strong and courageous.*

EZEKIEL'S INSTRUCTIONS (3:4–27)

Mission to the Nation Israel (3:4–11)

Ezekiel's mission was to his own people—the Israelites. But once more, God warned Ezekiel of their stubbornness and refusal to listen (v. 7). God would likewise make the prophet "stubborn"—persistent in conveying His message to the depraved nation (v. 8). This was essential if Ezekiel was to stand fast in his ministry. But Ezekiel's persistence was also dependent on his taking God's Word into his heart (v. 10). With conviction concerning God's Word, he would stand firm and faithful in ministry.

Ministry to the Exiles in Babylon (3:12–15)

In a vision, Ezekiel saw God's glory, causing him to assume the attitude of God toward the sinful nation in being embittered and angry in his spirit (v. 14). In a similar way, the prophet Jeremiah was "full of the wrath of the Lord" (Jer. 6:11). Following his vision, Ezekiel came to Tel-abib—not the modern city, but a city by the Chebar River in Babylon where he would assume his ministry.

Ministry as a Watchman (3:16–21)

As a watchman guarded a city from physical danger, so Ezekiel was appointed a spiritual watchman over Israel. As a watchman, he was responsible to warn the wicked and persuade them to turn from their wicked ways. If the prophet failed to warn the wicked, God said, "his blood I will require at your hand" (v 20). The phrase meant the prophet would forfeit his

"Eat a scroll"

This is figurative language exhorting Ezekiel to assimilate God's Word (the scroll) into his heart. Ezekiel was to mediate and receive God's word for himself and then faithfully proclaim it to the Hebrew people. But the message he was to proclaim was a message of "lamentations, mourning and woe" (v. 10). It was a difficult message—a message of judgment.

A watchman's responsibility was to stand on the protective wall surrounding the city and watch for possible invaders. The physical welfare of the people was in his hands. If the watchman saw an invading army, he sounded the trumpet, warning people of an impending invasion (2 Sam. 18:25; 2 Kings 9:17–18; Ps. 127:1; Isa. 62:6). If he failed, he forfeited his life. Hab. 2:1).

life (Judg. 9:24). But if the prophet warned the wicked and they refused to turn, the prophet would not be held accountable.

Ministry in his House (3:22–27)

Although Ezekiel was called to a difficult ministry, God's guidance and presence were apparent: "The hand of the Lord" (meaning the Lord's empowerment) was on him (v. 22), "the glory of the Lord" was revealed to Ezekiel (v. 23), and "the Spirit then entered" the prophet (v. 24). He was spiritually prepared to serve the Lord. But God placed a restriction on him—he would be confined to his house rather than being able to move about freely. The phrase "they will put ropes on you" is likely a figure of speech, indicating God Himself was restricting the prophet to his house (cp. 4:8).

Furthermore, Ezekiel would be rendered "dumb"—he was prohibited from speaking unless the Lord gave him a message (v. 27). The dumbness was not total but restrictive, as the Lord would direct him when and how to speak.

If we are to have an effective ministry that properly evaluates the people and their spiritual condition, we first must have God's perspective.

- Although the people were rebellious, God appointed Ezekiel as a watchman—he was to be faithful in warning them of their sin and urging them to turn from their wickedness.
- God would open Ezekiel's mouth, enabling him to speak to the people.

QUESTIONS TO GUIDE YOUR STUDY

1. What were the four living creatures Ezekiel saw in his initial vision?
2. What was the purpose of God's giving Ezekiel that vision?
3. What was the meaning of Ezekiel's eating the scroll?
4. What were the duties of a watchman?

SIGNS OF JUDGMENT (4:1–5:17)

God directed Ezekiel to use signs in conveying His message to Israel. These signs may be called "acted parables" since the prophet acted out the parables of the impending judgment.

Sign of the Clay Brick (4:1–3)

In this sign which symbolized Babylon's attack on Jerusalem, the prophet took a brick and drew on it a picture of Jerusalem. Then he placed the brick in the sand, built a ramp, and laid seige to the "city," complete with camps of soldiers and battering rams. The prophet himself assumed the posture of the Lord by setting an iron plate between himself and the city—indicating the people would not escape the attack—and looking with displeasure on Jerusalem. Ezekiel explained: "This is a sign to the house of Israel" (v. 3.

The sign symbolized Nebuchadnezzar's assault on Jerusalem 588–586 B.C.

Sign of the Prophet's Position (4:4–8)

In another sign to Israel, the Lord instructed Ezekiel to lie on his left side for 390 days for the sin of the house of Israel. When these days were completed, the prophet was to lie down on his right side for forty days for the sin of the house of Judah. During this time, Ezekiel was tied with ropes to restrict his movement. Ezekiel interpreted the sign: "A number of days corresponding to the years of their iniquity" (v. 5; cp. v. 6).

Many interpretations concerning the meaning of these numbers have been advanced. The 390 days may represent the period of time from the division of the kingdom in 931 B.C. until the end of the Babylonian captivity in 539 B.C.

11

The forty years may represent a round figure for the Babylonian captivity (figured from the final deportation in 586 B.C. until the return in 538 B.C.). Ezekiel's being tied with ropes represented Israel's inability to escape the captivity.

Sign of the Defiled Bread and Measured Water (4:9–17)

During the time the prophet was lying on his side, he took wheat, mixed it with other grains, and made bread. Normally, Israelites would use only wheat; mixing the wheat with coarser grains like barley was a sign of poverty and famine. Ezekiel weighed twenty shekels (eight ounces) of bread and ate it during the time he was lying on his side for 390 days. The bread was to be baked over human dung. Animal dung was commonly used as fuel, but human dung would have defiled the food (Deut. 23:12–14). When the prophet protested, the Lord allowed him to substitute animal dung (v. 15). The water he drank was also measured—approximately one quart (v. 11). The entire picture symbolized the scarcity of food because of the Babylonian invasion.

Shaving the head was a sign of mourning over death or disaster (Job 1:20; Isa. 15:2; Jer. 7:29; 41:5–6; 48:37; Ezek. 9:3). It symbolized humiliation (2 Sam. 10:4–5). The Law forbade a priest from shaving his head (Lev. 19:27; 21:5); hence, Ezekiel's shaving his head symbolized Israel's broken covenant with the Lord.

Sign of the Shaven Head and Beard (5:1–17)

God instructed Ezekiel to take a sharp sword. Using it as a barber's razor, he was to shave his head and beard. Then—in view of the people—Ezekiel burned one-third of his hair in the fire, struck one-third with the sword around the city, and scattered one-third to the wind. But Ezekiel took a few strands of hair and bound them in the fold of his robe (v. 3).

The acted parable is specifically interpreted in verse 12: One-third of the people of Jerusalem would die by the plague or famine; one-third would be killed by the invading Babylonian soldiers; and one-third would be scattered as they fled the devastated city. The few strands of hair in the fold of Ezekiel's garment represented the remnant that would be saved (6:8).

Verses 13–17 provide an amplified description of the judgment. Israel would be a symbol of warning to other nations. Through His judgments, God was displaying His wrath at sin and against Israel. The recurring phrase "I, the Lord, have spoken" reminded the people that their judgment originated with God (vv. 13, 15, 17).

■ *The acted parables of Ezek. 4:1–5:17 depict*
■ *God's judgment upon Jerusalem and the*
■ *nation through King Nebuchadnezzar and*
■ *the Babylonian army invading and destroy-*
■ *ing the city, killing many people and taking*
■ *the others captive into Babylon in 586 B.C.*

MESSAGES OF JUDGMENT (6:1–7:27)

Ezekiel delivered two messages of judgment: "The word of the Lord came to me saying" (6:1; 7:1). The phrase "you will know that I am the Lord" (6:7, 10, 13–14) illuminates the purpose of the judgments—it was to bring Israel to repentance and recognition of the Lord's disciplinary action.

Judgment Declared (6:1–14)

In announcing God's judgment upon Israel, the prophet assumed God's stern stance.

Ezekiel set his face toward the mountains, hills, ravines, and valleys of Israel (v. 3). The hills and valleys represented the places where the abominable idolatrous worship of Baal and Asherah took place. God announced that He would decimate the high places with the sword (v. 3) and

Knowledge brings responsibility. To whom much has been given, much will be demanded. There will be a greater responsibility on us who have received so much knowledge of the Word of God than on those who have little knowledge. What are we doing with the knowledge we have of the Word of God? Are we responding to it? Is it shaping our lives in godliness?

"Set your face"

The phrase "set your face" is used fourteen times in Ezekiel to indicate God's hostility toward sinful people (4:3, 7; 6:2; 13:17; 14:8; 15:7 (twice); 20:46; 21:2; 25:2; 28:21; 29:2; 35:2; 38:2)

desecrate the bodies of the idolaters by leaving them unburied in front of their idols (v. 5). When the altars were smashed and the people slain, they would know that the Lord had spoken in judgment (v. 7).

Yet God promised to preserve a remnant that would be scattered among the nations (v. 8). The remnant would be taken into captivity in Babylon—there they would remember their idolatrous practices, how they had sinned against the Lord—and they would realize the Lord had inflicted this judgment on them (v. 10).

In another visible display of God's displeasure against sinful Israel, Ezekiel clapped his hands and stamped his foot (v. 11), a symbol of joy (2 Kings 11:12; Ps. 98:8) or scorn (v. 11; 21:14, 17; 22:13; 25:6; cp. Job 27:23; Lam. 2:15). In this case, scorn was implied. Ezekiel explained the meaning: The people would die by the plague, sword, and famine because of their idolatry. The judgment would be thorough and complete; it would extend to those who were "far off" and those who were "near" (v. 12). It would encompass the entire land from the "wilderness" in the south to Diblah [this should probably read 'Riblah,' a town on the Orontes River in Syria] in the north—similar to saying "from Dan to Beersheba." None of the idolaters would escape God's judgment. And Israel would know that God is the Lord.

Judgment Described (7:1–27)
Judgment Pronounced (7:1–13)

In his second message of judgment (cp. 6:1), Ezekiel announced the impending and inevitable judgment by the fivefold use of "end" (7:2, 3, 6). Judgment could no longer be averted; it was certain. Ezekiel piled up terms of doom:

"An end! The end . . . the end . . . An end is coming; the end has come!" (vv. 2, 3, 6); "A disaster, unique disaster" (v. 5); "Your doom has come . . . The time has come, the day is near" (v. 7); "Your doom has gone forth" (v. 10); "The time has come" (v. 12). Judgment was around the corner.

Ezekiel again explained the reason for the judgment: "your abominations" (vv. 3, 4, 8, 9), a reference to their immoral idolatry.

"The day" of judgment was about to blossom like a flower (v. 10). "The rod has budded" refered to God's use of Babylon as His instrument of judgment upon the idolatrous nation (v. 10). Just as God had used Assyria to judge the Northern Kingdom (Isa. 10:5), so now God would use Babylon to judge Judah and Jerusalem.

With the unfolding judgment, normal social activity and commerce would cease; there would be no buying and selling (v. 12). Their belongings would become worthless since they would be confiscated by the Babylonians. But at issue was something more vital—their lives (v. 13).

Judgment Portrayed (7:14–27)

With the Babylonian invasion, there would be no escape. Outside the Babylonians waited for them with the sword; inside they faced famine and plague (v. 15). Outside the people would die by the sword; inside the people would die through famine. The few who would escape over the mountains would be left to cry out over their sin like mourning doves (v. 16).

Courage and morale would be gone in that day—"hands will hang limp, and all knees will become like water" (v. 17). In that day they would mourn by putting on sackcloth and

God speaks in the events of life. Just as God spoke to the Israelites in captivity, so God may speak to us in the events that transpire. What effect do our circumstances have on us? Do they harden our attitudes or make us bitter? Or do they cause us to develop humility and a contrite spirit?

Sackcloth was a rough, itchy cloth woven from the hair of goats. It was a dark material, fit for wearing on somber occasions since it depicted grief and sorrow (Gen. 37:34; 1 Kings 20:32; Isa. 37:1). Throwing ashes over the sackcloth emphasized mourning and self-chastisement (Isa. 58:5; Dan. 9:3).

shaving their heads (v. 18; Isa. 15:2–3; 22:12). Wealth would be worthless; they would throw money into the streets as though it were filthy—it could buy no food (v. 19). They had foolishly used their God-given finances to build idols (v. 20; cp. Hos. 2:8; 8:4).

The accumulated wealth of the people would be worthless since God would hand it over to the foreigners, the Babylonians (v. 21). Furthermore, God would allow the Babylonians to "profane My secret place" (v. 22), possibly a reference to the Holy of Holies, but probably a reference to the Temple itself. The Temple was the very place they had profaned with the introduction of idolatry. In 586 B.C. this prophecy was fulfilled when Nebuchadnezzar destroyed and burned the Temple (2 Kings 25:9).

In another acted parable, Ezekiel made a long chain, symbolizing the captivity of the nation and their forced march to Babylon (v. 23). The prophet continually held the nation's sins before them: "The land is full of bloody crimes, and the city is full of violence" (v. 23). "Bloody crimes" suggests they had committed sins worthy of the death penalty. For this reason, the Babylonians would possess their houses, destroy the Temple, and inflict disaster upon them. Instead of peace, they would experience painful exile. But God was dealing with them equitably, "according to their conduct" (v. 27).

N

- *In two major messages (6:1–7:27), Ezekiel*
- *indicted the nation for their idolatry and*
- *immorality. Because of their sinful practices,*
- *God was going to judge the nation by bring-*
- *ing the Babylonians into the land. They*
- *would destroy Jerusalem and the Temple,*
- *kill many of the people, and take the remnant*
- *into captivity in Babylon.*

VISIONS OF JUDGMENT (8:1–11:25)

Ezekiel had pronounced judgment upon the nation because of the people's sins. Now God transported Ezekiel in a vision from Babylon to Jerusalem so the prophet could see the abominable practices of the worshipers in Jerusalem and the ultimate judgment of God upon the idolaters.

Vision of the Sins in the Temple (8:1–18)

The "sixth year" was 592 B.C.; it was the sixth year after King Jehoiachin's exile (cp. 1:2). As Ezekiel was sitting with the elders of Judah, he saw the likeness of a man, illuminating with the appearance and brightness of fire (v. 2). This was a theophany—an appearance of God in human form. The brilliance also suggested the shekinah glory of God.

The key to understanding this section is the phrase "in the visions of God" (v. 3). Ezekiel was not physically taken to Jerusalem; he was supernaturally transported "in the Spirit" to Jerusalem (see note at 3:24). At the north gate of the inner court, Ezekiel saw the idol of jealousy, meaning it was an idol that provoked the Lord to jealousy. This may have been an idol of Asherah, the female fertility goddess, since King Manasseh of

The phrase "the Spirit lifted me up" does not imply an actual physical removal of Ezekiel. The phrase is explained in 8:3 where it says the Spirit lifted Ezekiel up and brought him "in the visions of God" to his appointed place. Similarly, it was in a vision that Ezekiel was transported to Jerusalem (11:1, 24); it was in a vision that Ezekiel saw the millennial temple (40:2; 43:5).

Judah had earlier placed an idol of Asherah in the Temple. The glory of God was there (v. 4), soon to depart because of the idolatry (10:18; 11:23).

North of the altar gate, where the animals were brought for sacrificial offerings to the Lord, there now stood the idol of jealousy (v. 5). After digging through a hole in the wall, Ezekiel saw pictures of rodents and animals carved on the wall (v. 10).

These creatures undoubtedly included some of the unclean animals of Lev. 11, in open defiance of the Lord. They also included the animal cults that were worshiped in Egypt.

The seventy elders present were not the Sanhedrin but leaders who represented the nation (Exod. 24:1; Num. 11:16). They held responsible positions, with oversight of political, judicial, and military matters. They were to uphold the Law for the people (Exod. 19:7; 24:1, 9–10). They failed dramatically, leading the people into idolatry. Furthermore, the elders practiced their idolatry in the Temple as well as in their homes (v. 12).

At the entrance to the north gate of the Temple, probably the entrance to the outer court, Ezekiel saw women weeping for Tammuz. This was one more example of the idolatrous abominations prevalent in Jerusalem.

Tammuz was the Sumerian god of vegetation. The people believed Tammuz died each year and descended into the underworld. The heat of summer and wilting of the vegetation depicted Tammuz's death. The people wept over Tammuz and in the spring, he emerged victorious from the underworld, bringing by the spring rains and emerging crops.

At the inner court, the court of the priests, Ezekiel saw twenty-five men bowing down to the sun in the east (v. 16). The twenty-five men were priests, made up of the twenty-four courses plus the high priest (1 Chron. 24:1–19). The Hebrew priests revealed their contempt for the Lord by turning their backs to Him in violation of God's Law (cp. Deut. 4:19; Jer. 32:33). The severity of this sin demanded judgment (vv. 17–18). God would deal with them in His wrath (v. 18).

N

- In his vision, Ezekiel saw the abominable
- idolatries in the Temple in Jerusalem and it
- encompassed all people: the civil leaders, the
- women, and the priests. Judgment was
- essential.

Vision of the Executioners (9:1–11)

The relationship between chapters 8 and 9 is evident: chapter 8 indicates the necessity of judgment; chapter 9 describes the judgment. Ezekiel 9 describes the judgment from God's vantage point; He is the One who judges the idolatrous nation.

God Himself summoned the executioners to judge idolatrous Jerusalem (v. 1). The six men were angels—God's messengers of judgment (cp. Gen. 19:1). They came from the north, the direction from which the invading Babylonians will come (v. 2). The man with a writing case was clothed in linen, symbolizing purity (10:6; Rev. 15:6). He is understood to be the Angel of the Lord, the preincarnate Christ.

From its place above the cherubim in the Holy of Holies, the glory of God came to the threshold of the Temple. Since true worship had departed from the Temple, the glory of God was departing from the Temple (cp. 10:18; 11:23). From the threshold of the Temple, God commanded the man with the writing case to mark the people in Jerusalem who mourned over the idolatry (v. 4).

The other six men were instructed to go throughout the city and slaughter the people who did not have the mark. The judgment was indiscriminate: old, young, women, and children.

Second Kings 24–25 describes the judgment from the human, historical perspective—the Babylonians invaded and destroyed Jerusalem.

The Hebrew word malak, translated "angel," simply means "messenger." Angels are God's divine messengers sent on a particular mission, sometimes to help and comfort (Gen. 18:1–14; 1 Kings 19:5–7; Luke 22:43) and at other times to judge (Gen. 19:12–13; Matt. 13:39–42; Acts 12:23; Rev. 14:4–18). Angels are frequently depicted as men in Scripture (Gen. 18:2, 16; 32:24; Josh. 5:13).

Ironically, the judgment began with the elders, the leaders who should have led the people in righteousness but who had led them astray (v. 6; cp. 1 Pet. 4:17). The bodies of the slain were strewn near the Temple, causing further defilement.

Fearful that not even a remnant would be left, Ezekiel cried out in alarm at the slaughter (v. 8). But the Lord explained the necessity of the judgment—the people had sinned greatly, the land was filled with sins deserving the death penalty, and the people thought God did not see their sins. Judgment was essential.

- *Because of the flagrant idolatry in Jerusalem,*
- *God judged the city. He spared the righteous*
- *remnant from execution but sent His divine*
- *messengers into the city to slaughter the idol-*
- *ators who had corrupted His holy name.*

Vision of the Coals of Fire (10:1–22)

The vision of chapter 10 relates to the vision of chapter 1. It is a reminder that judgment comes from the holy God of Israel.

The Lord judges Jerusalem with Fire (10:1–8)

During the tribulation, judgment will proceed from God Himself as He pours out His wrath on a sinful, hostile world (Rev. 6:16, 17; 11:18; 14:19; 15:1, 7; 16:1, 19).

From the glory of God in the Holy of Holies (v. 1) came the command to the man in linen to scatter coals of fire over the city. The coals of fire come from "between the whirling wheels under the cherubim." This was a continuing reminder that God was the One judging.

As the glory of God left the Holy of Holies, just before God's ultimate departure from the

Temple, the brilliance of God's glory filled the Temple court (v. 4).

Then God commanded the man in linen to take the burning coals. The cherub handed the coals of fire to the man in anticipation of the judgment on Jerusalem. Historically, this judgment was fulfilled in 586 B.C. when King Nebuchadnezzar and the Babylonians battered down the city walls and burned Jerusalem (2 Kings 25:8–10).

The cloud (v. 3) symbolized God's presence (cp. Exod. 33:9–10; 40:34–35; 1 Kings 8:10–11; Isa. 6:1–4; Ezek. 1:27–28).

The Lord departs from Jerusalem (10:9–22)
The description of the cherubim and the wheels repeats the picture of chapter 1. The additional mention of the cherubim and the wheels "full of eyes" is probably a reminder of God's omniscience (Gen. 16:13; Zech. 4:10; Rev. 4:6)—God saw the abominations of Jerusalem. The cherubim moved in unison, in preparation for the departure of the glory of God.

The glory of God departed from the threshold to the position above the cherubim. Then God mounted His throne-chariot for His departure from the city. The cherubim led the way out of the Temple to the eastern gate in preparation for the departure of the glory of God (v. 19). The eastern gate was the departure gate for the Mount of Olives. God was about to withdraw His presence and blessing from Jerusalem and the nation (11:23).

■ *With the judgment of Jerusalem imminent,*
■ *the glory of God prepared to depart from the*
■ *Temple. Because sin and idolatry were ram-*
■ *pant in the city, God withdrew His presence*
■ *and blessing. God and sin cannot coexist.*

"We are the flesh"

Lamar Cooper says of this enigmatic saying, "Most interpreters agree that the cooking pot, a clay vessel for cooking food, was used to protect the choice meats from the fire." [NAC, vol 17, p. 140]

While Ezekiel had been taken into captivity in Babylon, the prophet Jeremiah remained in the land ministering to the rebels in Judah and Jerusalem. In attempting to avoid God's rod of chastisement, the people in the land looked to Egypt for help instead of trusting in the Lord. Jeremiah rebuked the people for trusting Egypt instead of God and warned the people: Surrender to Babylon and live or resist Babylon and die in the city (Jer. 21:8–9; 27:11, 16–22; 38:17).

Vision of the Judgment and Restoration of the City (11:1–25)

Announcement of the City's Destruction (11:1–13)

The Spirit of God brought Ezekiel to the eastern gate, to the twenty-five men (not the same as in 8:16) who were the ruling elders of the nation's civil government. Instead of giving godly advice, they were leading the nation astray, giving evil advice (v. 3). What was their false advice? They were instructing the people to build houses—they were saying good times were ahead. They said the people in the land would not be taken captive; they should build their houses and the people who were already in captivity would soon return (Jer. 14:14–15; 28:1–11). They voiced a popular proverb: "This city is the pot" (v. 3)—we are protected from the fire of calamity; "we are the flesh"—we are valuable. They thought they were safe in the city. But they were lying to the people.

The Lord reversed the faulty saying of the people by informing them the slain who littered the streets of Jerusalem were the flesh (v. 7). The innocent people who had been killed would be the only ones who would remain in the city but the people who remained alive in the city—the pot—would be afforded no protection. The Babylonians would unleash their swords against them (v. 8, 10); God would bring them out and those remaining alive would go into captivity (v. 7). The city would not be a safe place; they would not be the "flesh," the "valuable ones" in the city. God was rendering judgment against them. When the Babylonians captured them, they would know that the Lord is God and that their sins had brought this calamity upon them (v. 12).

Announcement of the Exile's Restoration (11:14–21)

A prophet in Israel had a twofold message: For the sinful people in the nation there was a message of judgment for sin but for the righteous remnant in the land, a message of encouragement concerning the future. Ezekiel encouraged those captive in Babylon, as well as those of the Northern Kingdom who had been taken captive into Assyria in 722 B.C. ("the whole house of Israel," v. 15) —all those who had been ridiculed by the remaining people in Jerusalem (v. 15). God promised to bring them back from captivity in the future (v. 17).

The prophet Jeremiah was in the land, admonishing the people to submit to Nebuchadnezzar, king of Babylon, if they wanted to remain alive (Jer. 21:8–9; 38:2, 17). God was judging the people for their idolatry, using Babylon as His instrument of punishment.

Departure of the Glory of the Lord (11:22–25)

The impending calamity about to fall on Jerusalem became evident with the departure of the glory of God from the city. The glory of God departed to the east, lingering on the Mount of Olives as though waiting for the people to repent (v. 23).

Having witnessed the idolatry of the people and the resulting destruction of Jerusalem in a vision, Ezekiel conveyed God's message to the exiles in Babylon.

Although there was a partial restoration under Zerubbabel in 538 B.C., under Ezra in 458 B.C., and Nehemiah in 444 B.C., these verses look beyond those events to a final restoration of Israel to the land at the second coming of Christ and the establishment of the millennial kingdom (cp. 36.1–37:28; Deut. 30:1–10). In that future day, Israel would return to the land as a converted people, with a new heart and a new spirit (v. 19; 36:24–38; 37:11–28; Jer. 31:33; 32:38–39).

SN

- *The idolatrous people in Jerusalem had*
- *developed a false sense of security, thinking*
- *they were as precious as "meat in a kettle."*
- *But Ezekiel announced they would die by the*
- *Babylonian's sword and those remaining*
- *alive would be taken captive to Babylon.*
- *Anticipating the ultimate destruction of*
- *Jerusalem, the glory of God departed from*
- *the city. However, Ezekiel promised a future*
- *restoration when, in Messiah's glorious mil-*
- *lennial reign, they would have converted*
- *hearts of obedience.*

SIGNS, MESSAGES, AND PARABLES OF JUDGMENT (12:1–19:14)

In a series of signs, messages, and parables, Ezekiel continued his denunciation of the idolatry of the people, prophesying that the remaining people in the land would be taken captive into Babylon.

Sign of the Luggage (12:1–16)

To impact the people with His message, the Lord instructed Ezekiel to pack his belongings and prepare baggage for exile. The recurring phrase "in their sight" (vv. 3, 4, 5, 6) was designed to shock the people into the reality of the impending deportation to Babylon. In the evening Ezekiel was to go out through a hole he had dug in the wall (v. 5) and go to "another place" (v. 3). The people would understand the meaning of this since deportations had taken place earlier, in 605 B.C. and 597 B.C. Ezekiel was further instructed to cover his face so he couldn't see (v. 6). This acted parable was a sign to the nation (v. 6). Ezekiel did as the Lord instructed him (v. 7).

The "prince" is a reference to King Zedekiah, Judah's last ruler (597–586 B.C.). The interpretation is pointedly given in verse 11: "They will go into exile, into captivity." King Zedekiah would attempt to escape the city at night (v. 12), but he would be captured and blinded ("He will cover his face"). This prophecy was dramatically fulfilled when Zedekiah was captured and his sons were slaughtered before his eyes. With that as the last thing he saw, the king was blinded and carried into captivity in Babylon (2 Kings 25:6–7). Judah's military might would be ineffective; the remaining people would be scattered (vv. 14–15), but a remnant would be left (v. 16; cp. 6:8). This prophecy was fulfilled in 586 B.C. (2 Kings 25:1–11; Jer. 39:1–9; 52:1–11).

While the acted parable is described in verses 1–7, the interpretation is given in verses 8–16. The sign concerned the prince in Jerusalem and the house of Israel in the city (v. 10).

Sign of the Trembling Eater (12:17–20)

Ezekiel was instructed to tremble while eating his food and to shutter in fear while drinking his water. The interpretation of the sign is given in verses 19–20. The people in Jerusalem and Judah would tremble and shutter in fear while eating their food because the Babylonians would devastate the land and bring violence in their invasion. The people would experience terror—and they would know the Lord was speaking.

Message of Impending Judgment (12:21–28)

False prophets had nurtured a spirit of skepticism among the people. They had coined the proverb, "The days are long and every vision fails," suggesting the prophecies did not come true (see 2 Pet. 3:3–4).

Using flattering words (v. 24), these false prophets were telling the people there would be no Babylonian invasion and no captivity in Babylon (cp. Jer. 8:11; 14:13–14; 28:1–11). But God promised to put an end to these false sayings. The days for captivity were drawing near and the prophecies of judgment concerning the Babylonian invasion would be fulfilled (v. 23). The false visions, deceiving the people, would come to an end as would their divination.

But God's Word would certainly come true—in this instance, the prophecies concerning judgment. His prophecies would not be delayed any longer. Since He is the God of truth, every word is reliable and will definitely come to pass.

"Know this first of all, that in the last days mockers will come with their mocking, following after their own lusts, and saying, "Where is the promise of His coming? For ever since the fathers fell asleep, all continues just as it was from the beginning of creation" (2 Pet. 3:3–4).

■ *Through the acted parables of carrying the*
■ *baggage through the hole in the wall and eat-*
■ *ing his food while trembling, Ezekiel por-*
■ *trayed the imminent captivity and*
■ *enslavement to Babylon, King Zedekiah's*
■ *blindness, and the terror in the land follow-*
■ *ing the Babylonian invasion. God's Word*
■ *would come true.*

Message Against the False Prophets (13:1–23)

The False Prophets Denounced (13:1–16)

What was the cause of the nation's spiritual demise? The problem was the false leaders, the false prophets and prophetesses who were proclaiming a lie. Ezekiel condemned the false prophets who spoke "from their own inspiration" (v. 2), who had "seen nothing" (v. 3), who spoke falsehood when they said, "'The Lord declares,' when the Lord has not sent them" (v. 6), who saw a "false vision" and spoke "a lying divination" (v. 7). These were false prophets, following their own cunning imaginations; God had never called them, and they led the nation astray. The false prophets were like foxes that built their lair and lived among the ruins (v. 4). They had failed to repair the breaches in the spiritual wall of the nation so that the moral wall was about to collapse (v. 5). They were intent only on their own advance.

"Hand" is a metaphor that speaks of the strength of God for bringing blessing on believers and judgment on sinners.

In verses 8–16 the Lord pronounces judgment on the false prophets. God's hand will be against them in judgment.

God rendered a triple judgment on the false prophets: They would lose their influence and honored position; they would be omitted from the register of God's people, which barred them from fellowship with God (Exod. 32:32; Ezra 2:62; Isa. 4:3; Dan. 12:1); and they would not enter the land of Israel.

The false prophets had cried, "Peace! when there is no peace." (v. 10). They were like those who whitewashed a wall that was ready to collapse—a reference to the impending destruction of Jerusalem. God would bring a torrent of flooding rain and hailstones that would destroy their whitewashed wall (vv. 13–14). The wall of Jerusalem, the city itself, and the prophets would soon be swept away in judgment by the invading Babylonians.

The False Prophetesses Denounced (13:17–23)

Ezekiel condemned the women, the false prophetesses of Israel who were guilty of practicing witchcraft or magic; most likely these women were witches. They sewed magic bands or charms on their wrists, suggesting the binding power of their sorcery (v. 18). They were draped from head to foot in a veil perhaps adding to the mystery of their witchcraft. These witches were guilty of pandering their perversions for handfuls of barley and scraps of bread (v. 19). But God promised to end their sorcery and witchcraft by tearing off their bands and veils. They perverted the truth by discouraging the righteous and encouraging the wicked (v. 22). In their judgment, they would realize that the Lord is God.

This is the only reference in the Old Testament to false prophetesses. Although rare, there were legitimate prophetesses or women functioning in a prophetic ministry (Exod. 15:20; Judg. 4:4; 2 Kings 22:14; Neh. 6:14).

■ *At the root of Israel's sin was the problem of*
■ *false prophets and prophetesses. The false*
■ *prophets had never been called of God; they*
■ *spoke from their own imaginations and for*
■ *their own material benefit. God had not spo-*
■ *ken through them. The false prophetesses*
■ *were witches who would be brought to judg-*
■ *ment for leading the people in error.*

Message Against the Elders (14:1–23)

Repentance may Avert Judgment (14:1–11)
With Ezekiel largely confined to his house (3:24), the elders of Israel, who were also in exile with the prophet, came to him to inquire about the future of Jerusalem and Judah. But God revealed the hearts of the elders to Ezekiel; they had set up idols in their hearts. They may not have been worshiping idols in a literal sense but in their hearts they had idols—either because of the Babylonian idolatry surrounding them or because they longed for the idolatry they had practiced in the land of Israel. In their present idolatrous condition, the elders would not receive the answers they sought; instead, God would answer them according to their idolatrous mind-set (v. 4). Their idolatrous thinking had estranged them from God (v. 5).

What was Ezekiel's message to the idolatrous elders? "Repent, and turn away from your idols" (v. 6). There is a play on words in the statement. The word *repent* (Heb. *shub*), means, "Turn and let yourself be turned" from your idols. Ezekiel's message reflected the common theme of the prophet—calling the covenant people to repentance to turn them back in obedience to the Law which bound them to the Lord.

The necessity of repenting and returning to the Lord is stated in verses 7–8. God promised to cut off anyone who failed to repent. He would make that person a sign and a proverb; people would talk about the disaster that had overtaken him (v. 8; 23:10; cp. Job 17:6; 30:9; Ps. 44:14; Jer. 24:9). To be cut off means to be killed. That person would not continue to live among the covenant people of Israel.

Furthermore, if a prophet was enticed ("prevailed upon," NASB) to respond to the elders and he did so, God would destroy that prophet because he demonstrated he was a false prophet (v. 9). This statement is somewhat puzzling but follows the thought of 1 Kings 22:19–23. While God is never the author of evil, as the sovereign God He controls all things whether through primary or secondary causes. The purpose for God's severe judgment is stated in verse 11—so that the nation would no longer be disobedient and defiled by their idolatrous sins.

Can Christians have idols? What did John mean when he said, "Guard yourselves from idols" (1 John 5:21)? Does the world cause Christians to become idolatrous?

Intercession will not Avert Judgment (14:12–23)

Some people falsely thought the remnant in the land would avert judgment. But their sin was so serious that God warned that even the intercession of Noah, Daniel, and Job would not avert judgment (v. 14; cp. Gen. 6:18; Dan. 1:8–13; 9:4–19; Job 1:1; 42:7–10). God cited four possible judgments He could bring on the people: famine (v. 13), wild beasts (v. 15), the sword (v. 17), and the plague (v. 19). In no case could Noah, Daniel, or Job intercede to avert judgment (vv. 14, 16, 18, 20).

But how much worse if all these potential judgments should fall on one city—Jerusalem! Yet God promised to deliver some survivors from

The mention of Daniel in this context is noteworthy. It demonstrates that Daniel was a contemporary of Ezekiel, supporting an early date for the book of Daniel which liberal scholars tend to date late.

Jerusalem into exile. While the "survivors" appear to be the godly remnant, the phrase "their conduct and actions" suggests otherwise. This phrase is used seven times, and in each case it refers to evil actions. When those in exile saw the sinful actions of the survivors from Jerusalem, they would recognize that God's action in judging Jerusalem was just.

- The elders came to Ezekiel for advice, but
- God revealed to Ezekiel that the elders were
- harboring idolatrous thoughts. The only
- remedy for their idolatrous thinking was
- repentance—turning from their idols. The
- idolatry in Jerusalem was so severe, so
- intense that judgment could not be averted—
- not even by the intercession of Noah, Daniel,
- and Job.

Parable of the Vine (15:1–8)

The Parable (15:1–5)

To illustrate Israel's unfaithfulness and worthlessness in failing to bear the fruit of righteousness, the Lord revealed the uselessness of a vine as wood. The vine could not be used for construction or as a peg to hang pots in a house. The vine was even less useful when it had been charred on both ends and plucked from the fire—suggestive of Israel's suffering at the hands of Nebuchadnezzar (2 Kings 25:9). The vine was useful only for producing grapes.

The vine was a symbol of Israel (Deut. 32:32–33; Ps. 80:8–13; Isa. 5:1–7; Jer. 2:21; Hos. 10:1). The vine symbolized prosperity, blessing, and happiness in the nation. As the purpose of a vine was to be productive and bear grapes, so Israel was designed to bear the fruit of righteousness. Israel's joy and blessedness would culminate in the millennial kingdom of Christ (Joel 2:22, 24; 3:18; Mic. 4:4; Zech. 3:10).

The Interpretation (15:6–8)

The Lord clearly interpreted the parable: As the pruned vine limbs that bore no grapes were cut off and thrown into the fire, so God had delivered the inhabitants of Jerusalem to destruction by Nebuchadnezzar (v. 6). The people would not escape the invading Babylonian hordes, who would pillage and burn the city (2 Kings 25:1–12). But the Lord again reminded the people of the necessity of the judgment—"because they have acted unfaithfully" (v. 8).

■ *A vine is useful for only one thing: bearing*
■ *grapes. Similarly, Israel was God's chosen peo-*
■ *ple designed to bear the fruit of righteousness.*

Parable of the Faithless Wife (16:1–63)

In this parable of the adulterous wife, God revealed the faithlessness of Israel.

The Unwanted Child (16:1–5)

Through this parable, Ezekiel made known to Jerusalem "her abominations" (v. 2). Israel is pictured in her infancy as a Canaanite by birth. "Your father was an Amorite and your mother a Hittite" is a taunt, a sarcastic statement, inferring the nation's depravity as though it were a heathen nation. When no one cared for the nation, God took her up (vv. 4–5). This description of caring for a newborn in eastern culture is one of the most complete statements in Scripture (v. 4). Upon birth, the child's navel was cut and the midwife salted the child's skin for antiseptic purposes. The child was washed, rubbed with oil, and wrapped in cloths for seven days. The process was repeated for forty days.

Instead of receiving normal care as a child, Israel was thrown "into the open field"— undoubtedly a reference to Israel's sufferings in Egypt (Exod. 1–12).

The Amorites were nomadic western Semitic people who lived east of the Jordan River and south of the Dead Sea. From there they made their forays into the land. They were an immoral people, worshiping Baal and Asherah, the male and female gods of fertility. Other nations referred to them as "beasts." The Hittites were a vast kingdom of Asia Minor, spreading from modern Turkey eastward to Iraq. They had a pantheon dedicated to a thousand gods.

The Unwanted Child Claimed in Marriage (16:6–14)

But God showed compassion on the suffering nation and made it live, probably a reference to Israel's phenomenal growth in Egypt. From a patriarchal family of seventy-five that descended into Egypt (Acts 7:14), it emerged 430 years later as a nation of more than two million (Exod. 12:37–38). Israel became numerous in population, "like plants of the field" (v. 7).

When the Lord saw that she was a young woman, ready for marriage, He spread His skirt over her (v. 8), symbolic of protection and care through marriage (Ruth 3:9). The imagery refers to the Mosaic covenant through which Israel became the people of God and was bound to the Lord by the covenant (Exod. 19:5). Israel became the wife of Yahweh, the Lord (Jer. 2:2; 3:1; Hos. 2:2–23).

The Lord provided and cared for Israel, His wife (vv. 9–14). He cleansed her (v. 10; cp. Exod. 19:14); He clothed His bride in embroidered, multicolored material worn by a queen (v. 10); He gave her beautiful bridal jewelry (vv. 11–12; Gen. 24:22), including a queen's crown as well as the finest food (v. 14). This may refer to the glorious kingdoms of David and Solomon when Israel's borders were expanded and worship became centralized in Jerusalem. The fame of the nation expanded to other nations (v. 14). As a wayward child advancing to a queen, so God had exalted Israel from a patriarchal family to a nation well known among the Gentiles.

The Unfaithful Wife (16:15–34)

In the imagery of the Lord as husband and Israel as His wife, the wife became unfaithful, committing adultery on the "high places" (v 16). In spite of the Lord's faithfulness, Israel spurned the Lord's lovingkindness and committed spiritual adultery. Israel worshiped Baal and Asherah on the hills, committing immorality in this degrading Canaanite worship. Israel further spurned God's goodness by taking the blessings from the Lord and offering them in idolatrous worship (vv. 18–20)—which the Law forbade (Lev. 18:21; 20:2–5; Deut. 12:31). The nation failed to remember her humble beginnings (v. 22).

The depth of Israel's depravity is seen in the Lord's statement of lament and horror, "Woe, woe to you!" (v. 23). Israel expanded her idolatry by raising pagan shrines on every street, enticing people to idolatry. The graphic "you spread your legs" is explained as Israel's foreign alliances in verses 26–29—which also led to idolatry and immorality (23:8, 17, 30, 40; Isa. 30:1–2; 31:1; Jer. 17:7, 11–15). Instead of trusting the Lord as her King, Israel sought foreign alliances for protection from enemies—a practice condemned by the prophets (Isa. 30:1–2; 31:1–3).

To overcome the Assyrian threat, Israel sought an alliance with Egypt (v. 26; 2 Kings 17:4; 18:21). For this reason, God stretched out His hand in judgment against the nation (v. 27). Later, Israel entered into alliance with the Assyrians (v 28; 2 Kings 15:19–20; 16:7–9), viewed as harlotry by the Lord since Israel had been betrothed to the Lord. Israel was an unfaithful wife. Finally, Israel entered into alliance with Babylon (v. 29; 23:14–17; 2 Kings 24).

In the continuing imagery, God reminded the nation that unlike the typical harlot who received wages, Israel bribed and paid her lovers. This is a

"High Places"

The "high places" were pagan Caananite centers of worship. A tree or a pole in the ground was called Asherah, representing the female goddess of fertility (Isa. 17:8; 27:9; Mic. 5:14). The worship site also had stone pillars called *messeba*, depicting a male deity (2 Kings 3:2). The high places were centers of immorality since their worship involved temple prostitution in simulation of what Baal and Asherah did in the heavens (cp. 1 Kings 14:24; 2 Kings 21:3; Isa. 57:3–12; Jer. 2:20, 23; 7:31–32; Ezek. 16:16; Hos. 4:13). The people thought Baal and Asherah produced the rain and abundant crops through their sexual union in the heavens. By simulating that activity, they thought they would ensure rain and a plentiful harvest. Child sacrifice was also practiced on the high places.

The "high places" refers to the hills where Israel worshiped. Before the Temple was built, there was legitimate worship on the mountains of Israel (1 Sam. 10:5, 10; 1 Kings 3:2; 1 Chron. 16:39; 21:29), but later Israel adopted the idolatrous worship of the Canaanites—the worship of Baal, Asherah, Chemosh, and Molech on the high places. Baal (the male god) and Asherah (the female goddess) were thought to engage in sexual union in the heavens with the rain and spring crops the resultant blessings. Hence, worship of Baal and Asherah consisted of temple prostitution, simulating on earth what Baal and Asherah were doing in the heavens. The worship of Molech involved sacrificing infants in the fire (v. 21; cp. 2 Kings 23:10; Jer. 32:35; Mic. 6:7).

Just as a prostitute was stripped naked and exposed publicly (Hos. 2:3), so Israel would be stripped and exposed (Lam. 1:8).

reference to the tribute in money and material goods which Israel was forced to pay to the nations with whom it formed alliances (2 Kings 12:18; 16:8; 18:14; 23:33; Hos. 8:9).

The Punishment of the Wife (16:35–43)

In judgment for her harlotry, God promised to bring Israel's lovers against her to expose her nakedness (v. 37).

The fulfillment of this judgment was realized in the Babylonian invasion under Nebuchadnezzar, who pillaged and destroyed Jerusalem and Judah (vv. 40–41; 2 Kings 24:10–16 [597 B.C.] 25:1–12 [586 B.C.]). This judgment was designed to curb Israel's idolatry (v .41)—a judgment that accomplished its purpose. When Israel returned from the Babylonian captivity, the nation had been cured of idolatry.

The Enormity of the Wife's Sins (16:44–52)

Israel's sin could be characterized by the proverb, "Like mother, like daughter" (v. 44). The daughter was Jerusalem (representing Judah); the mother was the pagan Hittite (v. 3) who gave birth to three immoral children: Jerusalem, Samaria (vv. 46, 51), and Sodom (v. 46). Just as her pagan mother and her sisters had been immoral, so Jerusalem was also immoral. Yet Jerusalem and Judah had exceeded her sisters, Samaria and Sodom, in sin. Although Samaria engaged in Canaanite practices (2 Kings 17:7–18) and Sodom was well known for its immorality (Gen. 19:1–29; Isa. 1:10; Amos 4:11), Judah's sins exceeded them both. When compared with Judah's sins, Samaria and Sodom appeared righteous (v. 51; Jer. 3:11)! Judah had received greater privileges—but greater privilege carries with it greater responsibility (Matt. 10:15; 11:24).

The Restoration of the Wife (16:53–59)

Along with the restoration of Samaria (Northern Kingdom) and Sodom, God promised to restore Jerusalem and the Southern Kingdom. The hope of future restoration and blessing is a common theme of the prophets (Isa. 11:11–16; 27:13; 43:1–44:5; Jer. 12:14–17; 46:26; Hos. 6:11). Although Sodom's destruction was complete (Gen. 19:23–26), God promised to restore "Sodom with her daughters," referring to Sodom and the surrounding towns. Before Jerusalem's sin became evident, she disdained Sodom and her vices; but when Jerusalem's sin was uncovered she became a reproach to the women of Edom and Philistia. Jerusalem would bear the penalty of her abominations (v. 58), realized in the Babylonian invasion in 586 B.C.

Samaria represented the Northern Kingdom, Israel, which began as a separate nation from the Southern Kingdom, Judah, when the nation split following the death of Solomon (1 Kings 12). The division of the kingdom occurred in 931 B.C. with Jeroboam I ruling as the first king of the Northern Kingdom. The Northern Kingdom never had a godly king. After two centuries of apostasy, God judged the Northern Kingdom by bringing the Assyrians against them, who took the people captive to Assyria in 722/721 B.C.

The Renewal of the Covenant (16:60–63)

Although Judah was chastened, the discipline was not permanent. God promised, "I will remember My covenant . . . I will establish an everlasting covenant with you" (v. 60), "I will establish My covenant with you" (v. 62).

The new covenant was the spiritual condition through which God would bless Israel in the future millennial kingdom. Through the new covenant, God would give Israel a new heart, inclining the nation to walk in God's ways (Ezek. 36:25–27). That would be fulfilled in the future millennial kingdom; then they would know the Lord is God.

The covenant that God would remember was the Abrahamic covenant (Gen. 12:1–3), which promised Israel a land (developed in the Palestinian covenant, Deut. 30:1–10), a seed (developed in the Davidic covenant, (2 Sam. 7:12–16), and a blessing developed in the new covenant (Jer. 31:31–34).

Parable of the Two Eagles (17:1–21)

This parable reveals King Zedekiah's rebellion by seeking an alliance with Egypt instead of

Is it possible to spurn the love and grace of God? How? John declared that we have received "grace upon grace" (John 1:16). God continues to supply grace toward us. We use it up and God supplies more grace. But can we become callous toward it? How can we guard against it? How can we avoid spurning God's grace and falling into sin?

"Riddle"

A riddle is an obscure saying that requires interpretation (see Judg. 14:12, 13, 15, 16). The saying is also referred to as a parable, which actually was an allegory, an extended metaphor with several points of comparison.

trusting God, resulting in judgment through the Babylonian invasion.

Ezekiel posed a riddle, which was also described as a parable.

The parable is stated in verses 1–10, interpreted in verses 11–18, and applied in verses 19–21.

The great eagle (v. 3) symbolized the mighty Nebuchadnezzar, king of Babylon (v. 12). As an eagle swoops down on its prey and carries it away, so Babylon would invade Judah and Jerusalem and carry the people away to captivity in Babylon. The great wings and long feathers referred to the power and expansive empire of Nebuchadnezzar, while the full plumage of many colors referred to his conquest of many diverse nations (v. 3). Lebanon referred to Jerusalem since the cedars of Lebanon were used in the construction of the Temple. The "top of the cedar" (v. 3) referred to King Jehoiachin, who was taken captive in 597 B.C. (v. 12; 2 Kings 24:8–17). The thought is expanded in verse 4.

The great eagle also took some seed of the land and planted it in fertile soil, referring to Nebuchadnezzar's setting up Zedekiah as a vassal king (2 Chron. 36:10–13). The fertile soil and abundant waters suggested favorable conditions under which Nebuchadnezzar allowed Zedekiah to rule (vv. 5, 13, 14). If Zedekiah remained subservient to Nebuchadnezzar, he would be allowed to reign in peace. The "low, spreading vine" suggested the humiliation of Zedekiah (v. 6).

The other "great eagle" (v. 7) referred to Pharaoh Hophra of Egypt (588–569 B.C.). Instead of submitting to Nebuchadnezzar, Zedekiah rebelled against the Babylonian king, seeking an alliance with Egypt to overthrow the yoke of Babylon—but the desperate act would fail (vv. 7–10, 15–17; 2 Chron. 36:13; Jer. 37:5–7). The prophet Jeremiah warned the people against trusting in an alliance with Egypt instead of trusting the Lord (Jer. 37–38). God would not allow the rebellion against Nebuchadnezzar to thrive (vv. 9–10). The "east wind"—the invading Babylonians—would bring destruction to the land (vv. 10, 20, 21).

What is the Christian's responsibility toward government? Read Romans 13:1–7. Are there exceptions? What if there is a conflict between obedience to government and obedience to the Lord? Read Acts 4:19, 20; 5:29.

Nebuchadnezzar invaded Judah and launched a seige against Jerusalem in 588 B.C. (2 Kings 25:1), breaching the walls in 586 B.C. (2 Kings 25:2–7). Ultimately, the reason for God's judgment of Judah and Jerusalem was their broken covenant to Nebuchadnezzar (v. 18).

■ *Because of Israel's idolatry, God would judge*
■ *the people by sending the mighty Nebuchad-*
■ *nezzar and the Babylonians against the*
■ *Southern Kingdom. He took King Jehoiachin*
■ *captive to Babylon in 597 B.C. and installed*
■ *Zedekiah as a puppet king of Babylon. When*
■ *Zedekiah broke the covenant with Babylon*
■ *and rebelled by attempting to forge an alli-*
■ *ance with Egypt, Nebuchadnezzar invaded*
■ *Judah again. In 586 B.C., he took Zedekiah*
■ *captive to Babylon.*

Parable of the Tender Twig (17:22–24)
But Israel's history was not destined to end in shame and defeat. In a corollary of the preceding parable, the Lord announced the glorious future of Israel. God would take a sprig from the top of a cedar and plant it on a high mountain. This parable is messianic, envisioning Messiah's

rule in Jerusalem, on the lofty mountain of Judah. The "shoot" hints at similar messianic references (Isa. 11:1; Jer. 23:5–6). The "high and lofty mountain" referred to Mount Zion, where Messiah would ultimately establish the millennial kingdom (Ps. 2:6; Ezek 20:40; 37:22). This sprig would bear fruit so that birds of every kind would nest under it, suggestive of the nations of the world benefiting from Messiah's reign (Isa. 2:2–4; Mic. 4:1–5; Zech. 2:11; 14:16–21). Then all the trees—all the nations—would recognize Messiah and His sovereign and righteous rule. The "high tree," the proud nation of Babylon, would be humbled and the "low tree," the humbled nation of Israel, would be exalted under Messiah's rule. And all the people would know that the Lord had performed this.

Message of Retribution (18:1–32)

The Complaint of the Exiles (18:1–2)

Ezekiel had been announcing judgment upon the nation, but the exiles were complaining that they were being judged for sin that was not of their doing. They even quoted a proverb to make their point (v. 2). In the proverb, the sour grapes represented the sins of their fathers; "the children's teeth set on edge" meant they were suffering because of their fathers' sins.

Principle of Judgment Stated (18:3–4)

Ezekiel corrected their false notion by the following thesis: "The soul who sins will die" (v. 4). Ezekiel reminded the people that they were suffering for their own sins; the soul that sinned would die. To die meant to die physically and to be excluded from enjoying God's blessings in the land—the place of God's theocratic kingdom.

The exiles who issued the complaint (v. 2) may have been thinking about Exodus 20:5. In this verse God said He visits the sins of the father to the third and fourth generations. However, Exodus 20:5 does not contradict Ezekiel 18. Exodus 20:5 deals with the natural outworking of a godless father—he normally raises godless children who perpetuate godlessness for generations (see Lev. 26:39; Jer. 16:11–13; Dan. 9:16; Amos 7:17).

The concept of "live" and "die" is both physical and spiritual. To live means to enjoy physical and spiritual life in God's theocratic kingdom; to die is to be excluded from both physical and spiritual blessings in God's theocratic kingdom (cp. 3:16–21; 33:1–20).

The Principle of Judgment Illustrated (18:5–17)

BY THE RIGHTEOUS MAN (18:5–9)

According to Ezekiel, the righteous man demonstrates his righteousness by adhering to the Mosaic Law—the Word of God. He does not participate in pagan sacrifices; he does not worship idols (v. 6; Deut. 12:13–14); he does not sin against his neighbor's wife (v. 6; Exod. 20:14; Lev. 20:10); he doesn't oppress others (v. 7; Exod. 22:25–27); he doesn't steal (Exod. 20:15); he feeds the poor and hungry (v.7; Lev. 19:10–18). The righteous man is conscientious in keeping God's Law.

BY THE WICKED SON (18:10–13)

But the righteous man may have a violent son who sheds blood. He commits murder and keeps none of the precepts of the righteous man (vv. 5–9). He violates the word of God (vv. 10–13). What will be the result? "He will not live!" (v. 13). He will not benefit from the righteousness of his father; he will die for his own sin. "His blood will be on his own head" infers he has committed sins worthy of death (v. 13). The truth is obvious: The righteousness of the father is not transmitted to the son. The father will live because of his righteousness, and the son will die because of his unrighteousness.

BY THE RIGHTEOUS GRANDSON (18:14–18)

In the third generation, the son observes the wickedness of his father, and "does not do

"Justice, and only justice, you shall pursue, that you may live and possess the land which the Lord your God is giving you" (Deut. 16:20).

"See, I have set before you today life and prosperity, and death and adversity; in that I command you today to love the Lord your God, to walk in His ways and to keep His commandments and His statutes and His judgments, that you may live and multiply, and that the Lord your God may bless you in the land where you are entering to possess it" (Deut. 30:15–16).

likewise" (v. 14). He, like his grandfather, does not violate God's Law but rather obeys it (vv. 15–17; 18:5–9). What judgment is determined upon him? "He will surely live" (v. 17). The principle of individual judgment is enunciated once more: the grandson, in observing the sins of his father, determines to live righteously. He will live. God judges people individually.

The Principle of Judgment Summarized (18:19–20)

Verses 19–20 repeat the thought, with verse 20 summarizing the chapter: A son will not be punished for his father's sins, and a father will not bear the sins of the son. The righteous man lives by his righteousness and the wicked man dies because of his wickedness.

The Principle of Judgment Elaborated (18:21–32)

But the path of the righteous and the path of the wicked are not unalterable. Ezekiel cited examples of those who would turn from their original state. If a wicked man turned from his sins and practiced righteousness, he would live (v. 21). His sins would not be counted against him. Why is this so? Verse 23 explains—God does not take pleasure in the death of the wicked (cp. 1 Tim. 2:4; 2 Pet. 3:9).

"[God] who desires all men to be saved and to come to the knowledge of the truth" (1 Tim. 2:4).

"The Lord is not slow about His promise, as some count slowness, but is patient toward you, not wishing for any to perish but for all to come to repentance" (2 Pet. 3: 9).

Conversely, if a righteous man turns from righteousness to a life of wickedness, he will die (v. 24). All his righteous deeds will not be remembered; he will die because of his wickedness. What is the point? It is summarized in verse 26: He dies because of his sin. And when a wicked man turns from his wicked ways to righteousness, he will live "because he considered and turned away from all his transgressions" (v. 28). Death means exclusion from the blessing of living in the land; loss of salvation is not inferred.

The conclusion is given in 18:30–32—it is an exhortation to repentance. If people repent, their sins will not be a stumbling block to them—their sins will not incur their death. The call to a "new heart and a new spirit" is a call to salvation (cp. 36:25–27) and is the Old Testament equivalent of John 3:3, 5. God invites unbelievers to repent because God does not take pleasure in the death of the wicked (v. 32).

■ *God judges people individually. Children*
■ *will not be judged for the sins of their par-*
■ *ents, but neither will the righteousness of*
■ *parents be imputed to children. The one who*
■ *sins will die. But if a sinner repents and turns*
■ *from wickedness, God will not remember his*
■ *or her sins because God does not take plea-*
■ *sure in the death of the wicked.*

Lamentation for the Kings of Israel (19:1–14)

This chapter takes up a lamentation for the "princes" (kings) of Judah that had been taken captive into Egypt and Babylon. The chapter is set in a mournful poetic style with a 3 – 2 beat that is not readily noticeable in the English translation. Verse 3 does reflects this somber mood somewhat:

When she brought up / one / of her cubs

He became / a lion

And he learned / to tear / his prey

He devoured / men.

Ezekiel did not teach salvation by works. Salvation in every age is by God's grace through faith (Gen. 15:6; Hab. 2:4; John 3:16; Eph. 2:8–9). Works are always the *result* of salvation as well as the evidence of salvation. Works follow salvation, but they do not produce salvation. Neither does this chapter teach loss of salvation once a person has been saved. Salvation is secure for the believer (John 10:28–29). But God may judge the wayward through physical death (cp. 1 Cor. 11:30; 1 John 5:16).

How important is it that we demonstrate our faith by our works? Study Matthew 7:15–23 and James 2:20. Do these verses contradict Ephesians 2:8–9? See Ephesians 2:10. Can people who claim to be Christians but who do not give evidence of their faith through good works have assurance of salvation?

Jehoahaz reigned only three months before Pharaoh Neco captured him and imprisoned him in Egypt in 609 B.C. (2 Kings 23:31–34). A ring was hooked through his nose, then attached with a rope to a hook in the buttocks of the prisoner in front. The prisoners were marched—naked and attached to each other in this fashion into captivity (cp. Isa. 37:29).

Jehoahaz is taken captive to Egypt (19:1–4)

Set in metaphorical language, this chapter depicts the kings of Judah. The nation and the kingly line of Judah are portrayed as a lion (Gen. 49:9; Num. 23:24; 24:9; Mic. 5:8). The lioness (v. 2) probably refers to the nation that brought forth the kings; the lion cubs (v. 2) are the kings in the Davidic line; the lion that tore his prey (v. 3) is King Jehoahaz.

Jehoiachin is taken captive to Babylon (19:5–9)

Jehoiakim, who reigned 609–598 B.C., succeeded Jehoahaz (2 Kings 23:36; 24:6), but is not mentioned by Ezekiel. Jehoiakim was succeeded by his son, Jehoiachin (2 Kings 24:8–16). An evil king who also reigned only three months (598/597 B.C.), he was put in a cage with hooks and taken captive into Babylon by Nebuchadnezzar (v. 9). The cage was a further humiliation, the prisoner being subjected to public spectacle. Following thirty-seven years of imprisonment in Babylon, Jehoiachin was released, and he lived the remainder of his days in Babylon (2 Kings 25:27–30).

Zedekiah is taken captive to Babylon (19:10–14)

The figure changes to horticulture with King Zedekiah compared to a vine, a common metaphor for Israel (15:1–5; 17:1–10; Ps. 80:8–16; Isa. 5:1–2). The fruitful vine filled with strong branches probably referred to Israel's glory under David and Solomon, who expanded Israel's territory tenfold from the borders of Saul's kingdom (vv. 10–11; cp. 2 Sam. 8:1–18). The "east wind" that dried up the uprooted vine suggested the Babylonian invasions and devastation of the land, with the Babylonian captivity in view in the phrase "planted in the wilderness"

(v. 13). The branch that had been consumed by fire illustrated Zedekiah's capture and deportation to Babylon (2 Kings 25:1–12). The chapter is summarized by Ezekiel's reminder that "this is a lamentation" because of the collapse of the Judean kingdom (v. 14). It ended as it started—on a mournful note.

- *The chapter overviews the final kings of the*
- *Judean kingdom, with Jehoahaz being taken*
- *captive into Egypt and Jehoiachin and Zede-*
- *kiah being taken captive, like animals, into*
- *Babylon. The glory of Israel's kingdom,*
- *established under David and Solomon, was*
- *snuffed out with the Babylonian captivity.*
- *The restoration of Israel's kingdom awaited*
- *Messiah's return.*

FINAL PREDICTIONS OF JUDGMENT ON JERUSALEM (20:1–24:27)

Review of Israel's Unfaithfulness (20:1–32)
Israel's Rebellion in Egypt (20:1–8)

About eleven months following their previous visit (8:1), the elders of Israel again came to Ezekiel, seeking a revelation from the Lord. They were probably wondering about the duration of Israel's captivity. This visit occurred in the fifth month of the seventh year, July–August, 591 B.C. But because of their idolatrous practices, God refused to respond to the elders (v. 3, 31; cp. 14:3); instead, the Lord instructed Ezekiel to speak a twofold message to them: He was to remind them of their sins and continuing rebellion (vv. 4, 8, 13, 21), and he was to review God's patience in drawing them to Himself (vv. 9, 14, 21).

The five final kings of Judah were (2 Kings 22–25):

Josiah, good king, ruled 640–609 B.C., killed in battle by Pharaoh Neco.

Jehoahaz, evil king, ruled three months in 609 B.C., taken captive into Egypt.

Jehoiakim, evil king, ruled 609–598 B.C., died before he was captured.

Jehoiachin, evil king, ruled three months 598/597 B.C., taken captive into Babylon.

Zedekiah, evil king, ruled 597–586 B.C., taken captive into Babylon.

In faithfulness, God rescued the Israelites from bondage in Egypt and swore to bring them into a land of abundance—flowing with milk and honey (v. 6). But they continued to rebel against the Lord, defiling themselves with Egypt's idols (v. 7; Exod. 20:3–5). Their constant desire to return to Egypt may have reflected on their idolatry in Egypt (Exod 16:3; 17:3; Num 14:2–3; 20:3).

Israel's Rebellion in the Wilderness (20:9–26)

In delivering Israel from bondage in Egypt, God was acting for the sake of His name (v. 9). The surrounding nations would recognize His faithfulness and not profane His name. If God had destroyed Israel in the wilderness when they rebelled (cp. v. 8), the Egyptians would have accused the Lord of being unable to rescue the Israelites (v. 9; Exod. 32:12; Num. 14:16). But the Lord rescued them and entered into a covenant with them, giving them the Mosaic Law (Exod. 19), which promised spiritual and material blessings in the land (see Deut. 30:15–20). The Lord provided the Sabbath as a sign between Him and the Israelites (v. 12; Exod. 31:12–17).

But in spite of the Lord's faithfulness and blessing to Israel, they rebelled (v. 13). The rebellion is specifically defined as violation and rejection of the statutes and ordinances of the Mosaic Law by which Israel was bound to the Lord (v. 13; Exod. 32:1–6; Num 25:1–3). Israel deserved the wrath of God (Num. 14:11–12, 29). But the Lord acted for the sake of His name and did not destroy the nation (vv. 14, 17). However, the adult rebels who had witnessed the Lord's miraculous rescue from Egypt would not enter

"And I will make the land desolate so that your enemies who settle in it shall be appalled over it. You, however, I will scatter among the nations and will draw out a sword after you, as your land becomes desolate and your cities become waste. Then the land will enjoy its sabbaths all the days of the desolation, while you are in your enemies' land; then the land will rest and enjoy its sabbaths. All the days of its desolation it will observe the rest which it did not observe on your sabbaths, while you were living on it " (Lev. 26:32–35).

the Promised Land—they would die in the wilderness (Num. 14:20–30).

To prevent His people from following the evil path of their fathers, the Lord warned the second generation against idolatry and the evil ways of their parents (vv. 18–20). Just like their parents, the second generation also rebelled against the Lord and scorned His statutes. Once more God withheld His wrath and refrained from destroying them for the sake of His name, that it should not be blasphemed among the nations (v. 22). Nevertheless, God promised to punish the nation by sending them into exile into Assyria and Babylon (v. 23). Then the land would enjoy its Sabbath rest which Israel had neglected (Lev. 26:32–35; Deut. 4:27; 28:64; 2 Chron. 36:21).

Israel's Rebellion in the Land (20:27–28)

But Israel's rebellion and unfaithfulness extended even further. After the Lord brought them into the Promised Land, instead of worshiping God they resorted to idolatry (vv. 27–28).

Israel's Rebellion in Ezekiel's Day (20:29–32)

But the present generation could not escape God's indictment. Although the prophet had traced the history of Israel's idolatry and unfaithfulness in the past, Ezekiel demonstrated that Israel's pagan practices continued into the present (vv. 29–32). In emphasizing the point, the prophet presented a play on words: "What is the high place (Heb. *bamah*) to which you go? So its name is called Bamah to this day" (v. 29). Yet the elders of Israel had the presumption to inquire of God. But He would not hear them (v. 31). Instead, God would deal with their idolatry—"with an outstretched arm and with

The reference to the "high hill" refers to the pagan Canaanite sacrificial offerings on a large platform on a hill (16:24, 31, 39). This pagan worship which also involved male cult prostitutes (1 Kings 14:23, 24), divination and sorcery as well as the worship of Molech, with pagan worshipers sacrificing their infants in fire (2 Kings 17:16, 17). The "leafy tree" may refer to the worship of the fertility goddess Asherah, which was represented by a post, stake, or tree (Deut. 16:21; Isa. 17:8; 27:9).

wrath." He would deal with them in discipline and judgment to eradicate the idolatry. He would be their King!

It is easy to forget God's past blessings to us. Reflect on God's goodness to you in the past. List the ways He has answered your prayers, provided for you, blessed you, and encouraged you. Share these wonderful reminders with others.

■ *In a sad review of Israel's sordid history, God*
■ *revealed Israel's continuing apostasy and*
■ *idolatry. God rescued the people from Egypt,*
■ *but they held on to Egypt's idols; God sus-*
■ *tained them in the desert and entered into a*
■ *covenant with them by giving them the Law,*
■ *but they rejected the Lord and profaned His*
■ *revelation. Israel's rebellion persisted to the*
■ *present. As a result, God warned that He*
■ *would send them into captivity in Babylon.*

Revelation of God's Future Dealings (20:33–44)

In a final act of God's disciplinary judgment on the nation, God promised He would bring them "into the wilderness of the peoples" (v. 35). This referred to Israel's scattering among the gentile nations during the tribulation (cp. Rev. 12:14). There God would enter into judgment with Israel, making them "pass under the rod" (v. 37), separating the godly from the wicked as a faithful shepherd watches over his sheep (see Jer. 33:13).

At the end of the tribulation, the Lord will separate believing Israel from unbelieving Israel, not permitting the rebels to enter the millennial kingdom of Christ (cp. Matt. 25:1–30). Although they would persist in their idolatry in the present, the remnant would ultimately repent (v. 39).

With the nation purged of the rebellious, Israel on that future day would worship the Lord "on My holy mountain"—Zion, the city of Jerusalem (v. 40). With purified hearts (36:25–27), the reunited nation of Israel would serve the Lord. The repentant Israelites would be regathered from the nations where they had been scattered (Matt. 24:30–31; Isa. 27:13) and they would come back to the land in faith and knowledge of the Lord (vv. 42, 44).

Retribution on Apostate Israel (20:45–21:32)

Sign of the Forest Fire (20:45–49)

The sign of the forest fire parallels the sign of the drawn sword in chapter 21. Both signs dealt with the Babylonian invasion of Judah in 586 B.C. Ezekiel employed three words for the south in announcing the impending judgment. "Teman" means the right as one looks toward the east (47:19); the second term is translated "south," while the third word is "Negev," meaning the desert region to the south (Josh. 15:21). Because of the vast desert to the east, invaders would follow the fertile crescent, invading Israel from the north. The south thus represented Judah and Jerusalem (21:2). Ezekiel prophesied that Nebuchadnezzar would invade the land, which was to the south as he entered the land from the north. The invasion is described as a fire that would consume the trees. Some suggest the green tree referred to the righteous in the land, while the dry tree referred to the unrighteous (cp. 21:3, 4), suggesting everyone in the land would be affected.

Sign of the Drawn Sword (21:1–32)

THE SWORD DIRECTED AGAINST JERUSALEM (21:1–7)

Nebuchadnezzar destroyed the major public buildings of Jerusalem, demolished the city's walls, and carried the Temple treasures back to Babylon (2 Kings 25:1–17).

The sign of the drawn sword clarified and explained the previous sign. The south (20:46) was identified as Jerusalem and the sanctuaries (21:2); the fire (20:47) was the sword of Nebuchadnezzar (21:3), who was also identified as the king of Babylon (21:19). The green and dry trees (20:47) referred to the righteous and the wicked people (21:4). Nebuchadnezzar would be indiscriminate in destruction.

THE SWORD SHARPENED FOR SLAUGHTER (21:8–13)

To intensify the drama of the invasion, Ezekiel uttered a lament in poetic form, describing the invasion (vv. 8, 9). The repetition "a sword, a sword" dramatized the invasion; the sharpened sword would expedite the slaughter (v. 10), while the polished sword would incite fear among the people. To further express the horror of the invasion and slaughter Ezekiel was instructed to "cry out and wail" and strike his thigh, a symbol of mourning (v. 13; Jer. 31:19).

THE SWORD TRIPLED IN INTENSITY (21:14–17)

The intensity of the Babylonian invasion and subsequent slaughter is reflected in the phrase "let the sword be doubled the third time" (v. 14). Ezekiel clapped his hands together—as did the Lord—in expressing agreement with the judgment that was taking place (vv. 14, 17).

THE SWORD WIELDED BY NEBUCHADNEZZAR (21:18–32)

Against Jerusalem (21:18–27)

Rabbah was at the site of present-day Amman, Jordan.

To aid the invading Babylonians, the Lord instructed Ezekiel to sketch a road guiding the invading Nebuchadnezzar. At a fork in the road he was to make a signpost, directing Nebuchadnezzar into the land. One fork would lead to Rabbah; the other fork would lead to Jerusalem. Upon arriving at the fork in the road, Nebuchadnezzar would resort to divination to determine the right way, but God would control the divination, directing Nebuchadnezzar to Jerusalem (v. 22). With the capital of Judah at hand, the Babylonian king readied his military offensive against the holy city with a battle cry and battering rams as he prepared to lay siege to the city (v. 22).

In their false security the Israelites refused to believe the invasion was coming (v. 23). But it was coming—because they had broken their covenant through sin. They would be "seized with the hand" and forcibly captured by King Nebuchadnezzar.

A glimmer of hope is given in the phrase, "Until he comes whose right it is" (v. 27). It is a prohecy of Israel's future restoration under Messiah (cp. Gen. 49:10). Israel's humiliation would prevail until Messiah's return to rescue the suffering nation (Zech. 14:1–4; Matt. 24:29–31).

Against Ammon (21:28–32)

Since the Ammonites aided Babylon in their destruction of Jerusalem (2 Kings 24:2), God would later bring the Babylonians against Ammon (cp. Ezek. 25:1–7). In language similar to verses 9–10, the Babylonian sword would also be swift and effective in the destruction of the Ammonites. Ezekiel warned the Ammonites not to be deceived by false assurances; they would take their place with the wicked already slain in Judah. Resistance would be futile (v. 30). Although Nebuchadnezzar was the instrument of judgment, God was judging the sinful nation, symbolized by fire—expressive of God's wrath (vv. 31–32; cp. 20:47; 21:19).

The divination mentioned in verse 22 reflects its use in different countries. Arabs marked arrows, placed them in a container, and shook it until one was chosen or fell out; the household idols (*teraphim*) at times were carried along to ensure good fortune (Gen. 31:19; Judges 17:5; 1 Sam. 19:13, 16). Since the liver was considered the seat of life, the livers of sacrificial sheep were examined for an omen from a deity.

The Ammonites were a nomadic tribe that descended from Lot through his incestuous relationship with his daughter (Gen. 19:36–38). The Ammonites originally controlled the territory between the Arnon and Jabbok Rivers (Deut. 2:16–25; Judg. 11:13) but were later displaced by the Amorites, forcing the Ammonites to move east of the Jabbok River. The Ammonites worshiped Molech (also called Milcom; 1 Kings 11:5, 7, 33).

$\mathbf{S_N}$

- *In symbolic language of a drawn sword*
- *sharpened for slaughter, Ezekiel painted a*
- *horrifying picture of the destruction of Jerus-*
- *alem and Judah by the invading Babylo-*
- *nians. The Babylonians were God's*
- *instruments of judgment against Judah*
- *because of the nation's wickedness. And the*
- *Ammonites to the east would not be spared;*
- *they would also be judged.*

Indictment of Judah for Her Sins (22:1–31)

Cause of the Judgment (22:1–12)

In chapter 21, Ezekiel had described Judah's judgment; in chapter 22, he explained the reason for the judgment—because of the nation's sins.

Jerusalem was labeled "the bloody city" (vv. 2–4, 6, 9, 12–13; 24:6, 9) because of its violent crimes (7:23; 9:9; 24:6, 9; 33:25) and because of child sacrifice to Molech (16:20–21; 23:37, 39; 36:18). As a result, God would judge the city so it would be a city scorned by the nations (vv. 4, 5; cp. 21:4; Lev. 26:33; Deut. 28:64–68).

Ezekiel specifically condemned the nation for its violation of the Mosaic Covenant by which it was bound to the Lord (vv. 6–12). They violated the Sixth Commandment by scorning father and mother (v. 7; Exod. 20:12); they broke the First Commandment by despising the sacred things of the Temple (v. 8; Exod. 20:3); they broke the Fourth Commandment by profaning the Sabbath (v. 8; Exod. 20:8–11); they committed murder and adultery, breaking the Sixth And Seventh Commandments (vv. 9–10; Exod. 20:13, 14; cp. Lev. 18:19); they broke the Tenth Commandment by sinning with the neighbor's wife or daughter-in-law (v. 11; Exod. 20:17); they broke the Eighth And Ninth Commandments by taking bribes and bearing false witness (v. 12; Exod. 20:15, 16). And as a result of their sin, they had forgotten God—and violated the heart of the Law (Exod. 20:2–3).

Necessity of Judgment (22:13–16)

In a gesture of divine displeasure at their dishonesty and murderous deeds, the Lord asked the nation whether it would endure His chastisement. As punishment, the Lord announced that they would be scattered among the nations. This was fulfilled not only in 586 B.C. but also in the scattering of A.D. 70 with the spreading of the Jews to all the nations. The purpose was the nation's purification (v. 15; Isa. 4:4).

Smelting was the normal process for purifying metals by removing the dross. It was accomplished by placing the metal in a hot furnace. This figure is frequently used in Scripture for spiritual purification (Isa. 1:22, 25; 48:10; Jer. 9:7; Zech. 13:9; Mal. 3:2–3).

Purpose of Judgment (22:17–22)

Because of its sin, Israel was no better than dross—the waste material from smelting ore. To purify the nation, God made Jerusalem a smelting pot in which He would place the Israelites—the "bronze, tin, iron and lead"—and He would heat the furnace, removing the impurities and leaving the precious metal of righteous lives. Nebuchadnezzar was the fiery furnace which God would use to refine Israel. Then they would know that God had poured out His wrath on them.

Objects of the Judgment (22:23–31)

The cause of Israel's moral and spiritual depravity was the apostasy of Israel's leadership, and they, as well as the people themselves, would become the objects of God's judgment.

First, God indicted the prophets. Instead of warning the people and calling them back to obedience to the covenant (cp. Isa. 1:16–17), they were guilty of murder and robbery (v. 25).

51

The priests also, who ought to have instructed the people, profaned God's sanctuary by failing to distinguish between holy and profane (Lev. 19:8; 22:15, pure and impure (Lev. 10:10), clean and unclean (Lev. 11:47). The princes were also guilty. They were officials with the power of a magistrate (Exod. 18:21; Hos. 5:10; Isa. 1:23; 3:4, 14; 32:1). But instead of administering justice, they were guilty of murder, dishonesty, and destruction of other people (v. 27). Further, the prophets were guilty of religious "coverup," by whitewashing their sins with lies in claiming that God had given them their message when He had not (v. 28).

But the people were also guilty (v. 29). They violated the Law by oppressing others (Exod. 23:9), robbing (Exod. 20:15), and wronging the poor (Lev. 19:10,15) and the foreigner (Exod. 23:4–5).

What can Christians do to "stand in the gap" spiritually? What *should* Christians do? How should Christians be involved in society, in government, in "standing in the gap?"

When the Lord searched, He was unable to find a righteous person who would intercede on behalf of the nation. There was no one to build up the wall of righteousness—no one who would stand in the spiritual gap to prevent national ruin (v. 30). Therefore, God promised to pour out His wrath on the wayward, sinful nation.

N

- *God announced that He would judge the*
- *nation with the Babylonian invasion*
- *(chap. 21). Chapter 22 explains the reason*
- *for the judgment. Israel had violated the Law*
- *by which the nation was bound to the Lord.*
- *Moreover, the leaders of the nation—priests,*
- *princes, and prophets—were guilty of aban-*
- *doning and corrupting God's Word. For this*
- *reason, they, along with the people, would be*
- *scattered among the nations, beginning with*
- *the Babylonian captivity in 586 B.C.*

Parable of the Two Sisters (23:1–49)

In a lengthy parable, the nation is compared to two adulterous sisters, representing the Northern Kingdom (Israel) and the Southern Kingdom (Judah). Although the Northern Kingdom was taken captive into Assyria in 722 B.C., the Southern Kingdom did not learn the lesson and as a result was taken captive to Babylon in 586 B.C.

Identity of the Two Sisters (23:1–4)

The parable presents two sisters, daughter of the same mother (v. 2), suggesting a common origin through Rachel. Israel was born in Egypt, but this was also where they learned idolatry (Exod. 32:1–35). The phrase, "They played the harlot" (v. 3) denotes their idolatry which was, in effect, spiritual adultery.

Harlotry of Samaria (23:5–10)

Samaria's sin, described in verses 5–8, was that it "played the harlot" and "lusted after her lovers." Samaria, or the Northern Kingdom, trusted in the political alliances with the Assyrians rather than placing its trust in the Lord (Hos. 5:13;

"Oholah and Oholibah"

Oholah, representing Samaria and the Northern Kingdom, means "her tent," indicating Israel had set up an illegitimate worship center (1 Kings 12:28–29). Oholibah, representing Jerusalem and the Southern Kingdom, means "my tent in her," revealing that the authentic tabernacle of God existed in the Southern Kingdom (Judah).

The Assyrians worshiped a plurality of gods—about four thousand in number—that dominated the lives of the people. Their gods were related to wind, rain, sun, grain, fish, farming, dogs, fertility, and war. The people were subservient to the arbitrary will of the gods.

7:11; 8:9; 12:1). In order to form an alliance, in 743 B.C. Menahem paid tribute of one thousand talents of silver to the Assyrians (2 Kings 15:19–20). King Hoshea later also paid tribute to Assyria (2 Kings 17:3–4). Drawn by Assyria's wealth and power (v. 6), Israel also allied itself religiously with Assyria, worshiping Assyria's idols (vv. 7, 8).

But Israel's alliances led to its demise as the Assyrians took the Northern Kingdom captive into Assyria in 722 B.C. (v. 10). "They uncovered her nakedness" refers to the captivity (2 Kings 17:6, 23; 18:11). "They slew her" refers to the demise of the Northern Kingdom as a result of the captivity when it ceased to be a nation.

Harlotry of Jerusalem (23:11–35)

THE SIN WITH ASSYRIA (23:11–13)

Although Oholibah saw the sin and tragedy of her sister, she did not learn; she exceeded her sister in sin, also lusting after the Assyrians. This was a reference to King Ahaz seeking an alliance with Tiglath-pileser (2 Kings 16:5–10).

THE SIN WITH BABYLON (23:14–21)

Seeing the brilliantly colored images of the victorious Babylonians portrayed on the wall aroused Judah to lust for Babylon. The power and grandeur of the Babylonian warriors with their belts and turbans incited Judah to send messengers to Babylon (v. 16). As a result, Judah became defiled with her pagan alliance and consequently became disgusted with the Babylonians (v. 17; 2 Kings 24:1). Judah rebelled against Babylon, seeking help from Egypt (v. 19; 17:15; 2 Kings 24:20), only increasing its immorality. Driven by the sexual intensity of a horse and donkey in heat, Judah prostituted herself with Egypt (v. 20; Jer. 2:24; 5:8; 13:27; Hos. 8:9; cp. Exod. 32:1–10).

The punishment of Jerusalem (23:22–35)
The very nations that led Judah into idolatry would now become God's instruments of judgment against Judah. The invaders are mentioned in detail in verses 23, 24. The ancient Babylonians, Chaldeans (Neo-Babylonians), Pekod (an Aramean tribe of farmers), Shoa (possibly nomadic Arameans), and Koa (meaning is uncertain), along with the Assyrians who were assimilated into the Neo-Babylonian Empire, would join in the attack. These hordes would judge Judah according to their customs—and the Assyrians and Babylonians were well known for their brutality (v. 24).

Judgment of Jerusalem and Samaria (23:36–49)
Ezekiel pronounced judgment on Israel and Judah: They were guilty of adultery, murder, and idolatry—even sacrificing their children to Molech (v. 37; cp. 16:20–22; 20:30–31). Moreover, they had defiled the Lord's sanctuary and desecrated His Sabbaths (v. 38). "On the same day . . . on the same day" (vv. 38, 39) suggests that the day they committed adultery and sacrificed their children to Molech was the very day they also entered the Temple and pretended to worship the Lord. In this sense, they polluted and profaned the Lord's sanctuary.

As a prostitute plying her trade, beautifying herself for her lovers, so the nation (both Israel and Judah) entered into foreign alliances (v. 44; Jer. 4:30). As an alluring prostitute, these nations attracted the basest sort—a "carefree multitude" and "drunkards" (v. 42), representing the Arabs, Moabites, and Edomites. Thus, Israel's habitual

The term *Chaldeans* refers to the Neo-Babylonian Empire founded by Nabopolassar, the father of Nebuchadnezzar, after the fall of the Assyrian Empire in 612 B.C.

The Assyrians would remove the nose and ears of Judah, referring to their practice of mutilating an adulteress. Since the nose was considered the identifying feature of a person, invaders would remove the nose of a state to humiliate the people. The reference, of course, was to Jerusalem. Like an adulteress was mutilated, so Jerusalem would be destroyed and pillaged (vv. 25, 26, 29). Oholibah's fate would be the same as her sister's; she would drink the cup of God's wrath (v. 32). As Israel was taken into captivity to Assyria, so Judah would be taken captive to Babylon.

Someone has said, "One thing we learn from history is that we don't learn from history." The same could be applied to sin—we don't learn the lessons from the sins of others. We see the damaging results of sin: adultery, broken homes, divorce, and enslaving habits. Yet we fall into some of the same sins—with our eyes wide open.

degradation resulted in her being "worn out by adulteries" (v. 43).

Because of her continuation in sin, God pronounced the sentence: Righteous men would judge the nation. The reference was to the Babylonians, who as the instruments of a righteous God were termed righteous men (v. 45). Verse 46 explains: An invader will assault the city with stones—a reference to Babylon's catapults hurling rocks at Jerusalem. Once the wall was breached, the Babylonians would enter the city, slaughter the people, and burn the city (2 Kings 25:1–11). When these events transpired, the people would know that the Lord is God.

N

- *Likening the Northern Kingdom (Israel) and*
- *the Southern Kingdom (Judah) to two adul-*
- *terous sisters, the Lord detailed their apos-*
- *tasy in violating the Mosaic Covenant which*
- *bound them to the Lord. He depicted their*
- *sinful alliances with foreign nations, who*
- *ultimately became the Lord's instruments of*
- *judgment.*

Symbols of Jerusalem's Destruction (24:1–27)

The date of this prophecy announcing "the name of the day, this very day" that Nebuchadnezzar began his assault on Jerusalem is very precise—January 1, 588 B.C. (2 Kings 25:1; Jer. 52:4). Two woes are pronounced on the doomed city. The first woe describes the guilt and punishment of the people of Jerusalem (vv. 6–8). Two graphic parables depict Nebuchadnezzar's assault on Jerusalem (24:1–14) and the intense grief over the destruction of the city (24:15–24).

Parable of the Boiling Pot (24:1–14)

The date of Nebuchadnezzar's assault on Jerusalem is significant since it became a fast day (Zech. 8:19; cp. Jer. 52:4–34). Even though Ezekiel was ministering to the Jews in exile in Babylon, they too, like the people in Jerusalem, were a "rebellious house" (v. 3). In announcing a parable from the Lord, Ezekiel was instructed to put a pot of water on the fire, fill it with choice pieces of meat, and boil it with intensity (vv. 3–5).

With the parable given in verses 3–5, the interpretation of the parable is stated in verses 6–14. The pot represented Jerusalem, the bloody city, so called because it was guilty of bloodshed (22:1–16). The pot had rust that would not go away, representing the unbending stubbornness of the people. But now, the choice pieces of meat, representing the elite, proud people of Jerusalem, would be taken out of the city to captivity in Babylon (v. 6). In his earlier invasions, Nebuchadnezzar had taken the educated and the craftsmen from the city (2 Kings 24:14; Dan. 1:3–4); now there would be no consideration concerning the captives. But Jerusalem's sin and bloodshed lay as though exposed on a rock, declared guilty and crying for vengeance like the blood of Abel (Gen 4:10; cp. Job 16:18; Isa. 26:21).

The second woe describes the intensity of the judgment (vv. 9–14). The wood would be piled high, intensifying the heat; the meat in the pot would be boiled thoroughly (lit., "completely," v. 10). Then the empty pot would be set on the glowing coals to remove all its impurities in this smelting process (v. 11). Nebuchadnezzar was the human instrument God was using to purify Judah and Jerusalem. Nebuchadnezzar's three

Who is the object of God's wrath today? Are believers the objects of God's wrath? Study Romans 5:1, 9; 1 Thess 1:10; 5:9. How will God exhibit His wrath in the future? Study Rev. 6:16, 17; 11:18; 14:19; 15:1, 7; 16:1, 19.

Mourning at the death of a Hebrew loved one normally involved noisy lamentation (Gen 23:2; 2 Sam 1:12; Isa 22:12; Joel 2:12; Matt 9:23). The mourner also uncovered or shaved his head on which he scattered dust or ashes (Josh 7:6; 1 Sam 4:12), removed his turban and sandals (2 Sam 15:30; Isa 20:2), tore his clothing (2 Sam 3:31), and covered his face (Lev 13:45; 2 Sam 15:30; Jer 14:3). As an act of sympathy, friends would bring the mourner food (24:17; Jer 16:7; Hos 9:4).

invasions (605 B.C., 597 B.C., 586 B.C.) resulted in the destruction of Jerusalem and the Babylonian captivity where God would rid the people of their idolatrous practices.

Because of its stubbornness, the nation had wearied God (v. 12); hence, the fiery judgment was necessary to bring the stubborn nation to repentance and restoration.

The point of the parable is explained in verses 13–14. God would be wearied no more. Although He had dealt with them in grace by cleansing them, yet they had remained stubbornly entrenched in their sin. Now there would be no recourse—captivity in Babylon was certain. God would pour out His wrath on them and would not relent.

Sign of the Death of Ezekiel's Wife (24:15–27)

In the most painful acted parable Ezekiel was to portray, the Lord informed Ezekiel that his wife would be taken from him "with a blow"—suggestive of a sudden death. His wife is called "the desire of your eyes," revealing the genuine love and bliss in Ezekiel's marriage. But the Lord warned Ezekiel not to resort to the customary mourning when his wife died. Instead, Ezekiel was instructed to put on his turban and shoes, and not to cover his face in mourning. He was even to reject the meal of sympathy by friends (v. 17). He was to carry on his life as usual, without any outward mourning. He was to "groan silently," keeping his grief to himself (v. 17).

In the morning Ezekiel prophesied to the people that his wife would die and she died that evening (v. 18). But on the following morning, Ezekiel did as the Lord had commanded him—he gave no indication of mourning for his wife (v. 18).

The meaning of the death of Ezekiel's wife's is stated in verses 19–24. When the people observed Ezekiel's unusual behavior, they demanded to know why he wasn't mourning (v. 19). Just as Ezekiel's wife—the desire of his eyes—had been taken from him and he had not mourned, so the sanctuary—the desire of their eyes—as well as their children, would be destroyed and they would not mourn outwardly. There would be no opportunity for an outward display of grief. Instead, they would groan inwardly on their trek to Babylon (vv. 21–23). The destruction of the sanctuary would be a sign that God had spoken (v. 24).

Why do Christians suffer? Doesn't it seem unusual that believers should suffer? What benefits can God bring to believers through suffering? Study Job 1:1–2:10; Rom. 5:3–5; 2 Cor. 1:11; 1 Thess. 1:3, 6–10; James 1:2–4; Heb. 12:1–11.

The Lord told Ezekiel that on the precise day of the Temple's destruction, a fugitive from the holocaust would escape and bring the news to Ezekiel in Babylon (delivered six months later, 33:21). With the delivery of the tragic news, Ezekiel's ministry would change. His audience would become willing listeners and the Lord would open Ezekiel's mouth, giving him freedom in ministry by removing his earlier restriction (3:25–27). He would again speak openly as the people would recognize that Ezekiel was a sign to the nation, having spoken forthrightly concerning the nation (3:25, 27).

- *Because of Judah's continuing rebellion, the*
- *Lord announced, through the parable of the*
- *boiling pot, the destruction of Jerusalem.*
- *Like a fierce fire bringing the pot of flesh to a*
- *boil, so Nebuchadnezzar would assault the*
- *city in a fiery invasion, resulting in many*
- *inhabitants being slaughtered and others*
- *taken captive. When Ezekiel's wife died, Eze-*
- *kiel refused all mourning, reflecting the*
- *response of the people when the sanctuary*
- *and the city would be destroyed.*

QUESTIONS TO GUIDE YOUR STUDY

1. What prompted God's judgment against Judah and Jerusalem?
2. Who would be the instrument of God's judgment?
3. To what did God liken the Northern Kingdom and the Southern Kingdom?
4. What was God's instruction to Ezekiel when his wife died?

JUDGMENT AGAINST THE NATIONS (25:1–32:32)

God's judgment on seven heathen nations is detailed in these chapters. Each nation was in some way related to Israel: They opposed Israel and rejoiced when the nation was overthrown (25:3, 6, 8, 12, 15; 26:2; 28:24; 29:1–16). But God is sovereign over gentile nations as well as Israel, and He would judge them as well. Similar parallels exist in the Old Testament prophets (Isa. 13–23; Jer. 46–51; Amos 1:3–2:3; Zeph. 2:4–15).

PROPHECY AGAINST AMMON (25:1–7)

God indicted the Ammonites for their derisive rejoicing ("Aha") when Nebuchadnezzar ransacked and destroyed the Temple and devastated the land of Judah, taking the people captive to Babylon (v. 3).

As punishment, God announced He would give the land of the Ammonites to the "sons of the east," the Arabs who were descendants of Ishmael (Gen 25:13–18). The Arabs would occupy their territory (v. 4) and dispossess the Ammonites of Rabbah, then the capital. Instead of being a prominent city, Rabbah would become a resting place for livestock (v. 5). The Ammonites would be plundered by the nations and ultimately destroyed. They had clapped their hands in glee at Israel's suffering; God would raise His hand against them in judgment.

PROPHECY AGAINST MOAB (25:8–11)

Exhibiting their hatred of Judah (cp. Num. 22–24), the Moabites ridiculed Judah's unique relationship to the Lord. Together with the

Ammonite history began with the incestuous relationship between Lot and his younger daughter, who bore him a son, Ben-Ammi (Gen. 19:38). The Ammonites lived in the territory east of the Jordan River, between the Arnon and Jabbok Rivers. From earlier times the Ammonites exhibited their hatred of Israel by oppressing them (Judg. 10:8), suffering defeat at the hands of Jephthah (Judg. 11:32–33), warring against Israel in Saul's day (1 Sam. 11), being subdued in David's time (2 Sam. 10:1–14), and suffering defeat by Jehoshaphat (2 Chron. 20). More recently, the Ammonites had attacked Israel (2 Kings 24:2).

61

Moabite ancestry is similar to the Ammonites, since they descended from an incestuous relationship between Lot and his eldest daughter (Gen. 19:30–38). The Moabites lived between the Arnon and Zered Rivers east of the Jordan River.

The Edomites were descendants of Esau (Gen. 25:21–28), occupying the rocky, desert territory south of the Zered River and south of the Dead Sea to the Gulf of Aqaba. Hostility between the Edomites and Israel could be traced to the quarrel between Esau and Jacob over the birthright (Gen. 25:27–34). David defeated the Edomites (2 Sam. 8:14), who had earlier refused Israel passage through their land (Num. 20:14–21).

Edomites ("Seir"), they declared that Judah was like other gentile nations (v. 8).

Because of their sin, God declared He would give their frontier cities—along with their people—to the Arabs, the sons of the east (v. 10). Five years after the destruction of Jerusalem, this prophecy was fulfilled (v. 11). The Moabites, like the Ammonites, ceased to be remembered.

PROPHECY AGAINST EDOM (25:12–16)

Because of their hostility toward Israel in encouraging Babylon's devastation of Jerusalem (Ps. 137:7), God pronounced punishment on Edom (vv. 13, 14). From their city Teman in the north to Dedan in the south, they would be devastated—a prophecy that was fulfilled first when the Nabataeans occupied their territory and later when the Edomites became part of Idumea. Under Judas Maccabeus, the Jews defeated Idumea; and the Edomites were absorbed into Judaism losing their distinctiveness.

PROPHECY AGAINST PHILISTIA (25:15–17)

Because they sought to destroy Israel (v. 15), God promised to destroy the coastal people, along with the Cherethites—a synonym for the Philistines (and a fighting force formerly employed as David's bodyguards; 2 Sam. 8:18).

■ *Israel stands in a unique relationship to the*
■ *Lord. Throughout history, those nations that*
■ *vented hostility toward Israel have been*
■ *judged by God.*

PROPHECY AGAINST TYRE (26:1–28:19)

Destruction of Tyre (26:1–21)

The Prediction (26:1–6)

The prophecy concerning Tyre's destruction came in the eleventh year of Jehoiachin's exile, 586 B.C. Tyre's sin and reason for destruction was that it gloated over Jerusalem's devastation (v. 2; cp. 25:3, 8, 12, 15). Since Tyre viewed Jerusalem as a rival in trade, Tyre rejoiced at Jerusalem's destruction—now the traders formerly bound for Jerusalem would turn to Tyre for trade (v. 2).

But as the waves pounded the Tyre shoreline, so the invaders would pound the island city (v. 3). The anticipated traders would actually be conquerors who would destroy the proud city (vv. 3–4). All that would be left of the mighty fortress would be bare rock where fishermen would dry their nets.

The Destruction (26:7–21)

The invader is specifically identified as Nebuchadnezzar, king of Babylon, who would assault Tyre (v. 7). He would destroy the villages ("daughters") on the mainland and lay seige to Tyre—which Nebuchadnezzar did in 585–573 B.C. (vv. 8–9).

The pronoun shift from "he" (v. 8) to "they" (v. 12) suggested the devastation described in these verses would come at the hands of other invaders subsequent to Nebuchadnezzar.

The ferocity of the invasion would raise dust from the horses that would cover the city (v. 10). The city walls would shake and the pillars, perhaps the obelisks dedicated to Melkart, god of Tyre, would fall (v. 11). Tyre would be

Situated on the Mediterranean coast 25 miles south of Sidon, Tyre was a prominent commercial center and seaport with two harbors, one on the mainland and the other on an island, one and one-half miles off shore. Founded in 2740 B.C., Tyre was a prominent trade center. Hiram, king of Tyre, provided cedar trees and craftsmen for David (2 Sam. 5:11) and Solomon (1 Kings 5:1–10). Eventually, Tyre was controlled by Assyria, later attacked by Nebuchadnezzar, king of Babylon (585–573 B.C.) and eventually conquered by Alexander the Great in 332 B.C.

This prophecy was fulfilled when Alexander the Great conquered Tyre by building a causeway to the city and attacking it from both the causeway and the sea.

"Obelisk"

An obelisk is a stone pillar used in worship. Four-sided and made from one stone, obelisks tapered to the top, where a pyramid rested. At times, obelisks symbolized the rays of the rising sun. They were also used in tombs to represent hope for resurrection.

The pit (Heb. *bor*), as a synonym for Sheol, may depict the *state* of death (Ps. 88:4, 6; 143:7), or it may denote the *place* of judgment for the wicked (26:20; 31:14, 16; 32:18, 23–24, 29–30). Since the same term is also used of a dungeon (Gen. 40:15; 41:14; Exod. 12:29; Jer. 37:16), it is a suitable expression for a place of judgment.

Christians should never rejoice in tragedies of others. Believers are to "rejoice with them that rejoice and weep with them that weep." See 1 Cor. 5:2.

plundered of its wealth and destroyed (v. 12). Silence would replace its songs (v. 13).

The neighboring coastlands would tremble at the news of Tyre's destruction. The merchants ("princes of the sea"; Isa. 23:8) would lament Tyre's fall since they were economically bound to Tyre by trade. The lamentation (vv. 17–18) is written in the qina (3–2) meter, a mournful Hebrew poetry style.

The Lord announced the desolation of Tyre in verses 19–21. The city that had been exalted over the sea would now be submerged beneath the sea (v. 19). It would go down to the pit—a synonym for Sheol.

God would judge Tyre, resulting in a horrible and permanent destruction. The city would never be rebuilt.

■ *The great city of Tyre would be destroyed*
■ *because it reveled in Jerusalem's destruction.*
■ *Nebuchadnezzar, and later Alexander the*
■ *Great, would assault the city, resulting in its*
■ *obliteration.*

Lamentation about Tyre (27:1–36)
Greatness of Tyre (27:1–25)

Ezekiel took up a lament about Tyre in poetry form in verses 3b–9, 25b–36. Tyre was situated at "the entrance to the sea," the harbors through which the merchants sailed. Tyre boasted of her beauty—probably the basis of her sin (cp. 28:12). In the lament, Tyre is compared with a magnificently built ship (vv. 5ff.).

The ship's timbers came from Senir (the Amorite name for Mount Hermon, Deut. 3:9); cedar from Lebanon provided the mast (v. 5). The oars were constructed from the oaks of Bashan; the deck was of boxwood inlaid with ivory. The sail, serving as an ensign, was embroidered in colorful designs on fine linen from Egypt (v. 7). The deck awnings were of blue and purple from Elishah—Cyprus. The oarsmen came from Sidon and Arvad (Ruad), an island north of Tripoli. Wise men were at her helm; governors from Gebal (Byblos) provided advice when repairs were needed (v. 9). As a city, Tyre attracted the nations of the world (v. 9b).

Mercenaries from foreign nations guarded the city and its walls (vv. 10–11). They hung their shields and helmets in the city, symbolic of their protection of the city.

Tyre's widespread commerce is detailed in verses 12–25, beginning in the extreme west, then north, northeast, and finally Tarshish in the west again. Tarshish, meaning "smelting plant," and recognized for its abundance of silver, was a port in southern Spain (v. 12). Thirty-seven different products from these twenty nations are listed, emphasizing the magnitude of Tyre's trade. Commerce extended to Greece ("Javan"; v. 13), Tubal and Meshech, barbaric people living on both sides of the Anti-Taurus range in Asia Minor who used slaves for barter in Tyre (v. 13). Well known for its horses was Beth-togarmah (v. 14; cp. 38:4, 6).

Also included was Dedan, an Arab tribe in Arabia (vv. 15, 20), Aram (Syria) known for its textiles, and even Judah and Israel (v. 17). Damascus traded wine from Helbon (v. 18)—even Bedouin Arab tribes (v. 21) came to trade. Sheba and Raamah reflected the extent of Tyre's trade since they were over one thousand miles southeast of Jerusalem, in the southwest corner of Arabia. Even the cities of Mesopotamia came (v. 23). With goods bound for many nations, the ships of Tarshish were pictured transporting Tyre's products around the world (v. 25).

Picturing Tyre as a ship, Ezekiel described Tyre's destruction. Her oarsmen were depicted bringing Tyre into turbulent waters with an east wind, representative of Nebuchadnezzar, bringing about its destruction and an end to its commerce (vv. 26–28).

Is ambition and planning wrong? When can it become wrong? When does self-reliance and pride set in? Study James 4:13–17. What can we learn about planning from this passage?

The merchants who traded with Tyre would bitterly lament Tyre's fall (vv. 29–31). The intensity of their grief is reflected in the customary mourning rituals they displayed (vv. 30–31). Tyre was without peer in its trade, but now it is silent—like a sunken ship (v. 32). But Tyre's fall was not in isolation; kings and merchants that traded with her would suffer their own economic loss and ruin.

■ *Because of its commercial strength, Tyre*
■ *became proud in its global, commercial posi-*
■ *tion. Her traders were many, from around*
■ *the world. But Tyre would ultimately be*
■ *destroyed and her commercial enterprise*
■ *would cease—and along with it, many other*
■ *nations' commerce.*

Fall of the King of Tyre (28:1–19)
The Destruction (28:1–10)
God commanded Ezekiel to declare the sin (vv. 2–5) and resulting punishment (vv. 6–10) of the king of Tyre. He is addressed as "leader" (Heb. *nagidh*), a term sometimes used of Israel's

kings (1 Sam. 13:14; 2 Sam. 7:8; Dan. 9:25–26). In absolute arrogance, the king sat enthroned in his island fortress as though he was a god (v. 2)—similar to what the Antichrist will do one day (2 Thess. 2:4).

Like the king of Babylon (Isa. 14:13–14), the king of Tyre exalted himself as God—but he was just a man, and his demise would reflect it. The king saw himself as wiser than Daniel and assumed he had accumulated his wealth through his wisdom (vv. 3–5).

"I will ascend above the heights of the clouds; I will make myself like the Most High" (Isa. 14:14).

Because of his pride in likening himself to God, the king would have the most ruthless of nations arrayed against him—Babylon (v. 4; 30:11; 31:12; 32:12). The Babylonians would destroy Tyre's beauty, and the king himself would be brought down to the pit (v. 8). The king would come to an inglorious end, dying a violent death. In the presence of his slayer, his pride would vanish (v. 9). Although the king of Tyre had claimed deity, he would die like an uncircumcised barbarian (31:18; 32:19, 21, 24).

The pit (Heb. *shahat*) "came to mean 'the grave'—graves in those times were usually caves dug into the rock—and then was extended to mean the corruption of the grave. . . . It seems clear that sometimes *shahat* refers to the grave and its decay. In Job 17:14, it is parallel to 'the worm.' In Job 33:18–30, the subject is death by sword or disease. Psalm 16:10, like 49:9, refers to decay in death (cp. 49:14). Psalm 55:23 speaks of the 'pit of corruption' (R. Laird Harris, "shahat," *Theological Wordbook of the O.T.*, 2:911). See also Job 33:24, 28, 30; Pss. 16:10; 49:10).

The Dirge (28:11–19)

The language of these verses indicates that this discussion passed beyond the king of Tyre to a description of Satan, the power behind this king. The expressions "perfect in beauty" (v. 12), "Eden, the garden of God" (v. 13), "anointed cherub" (v. 14), "holy mountain of God" (v. 14), and "blameless" (v. 15) demand that this discussion move beyond the king of Tyre. This passage parallels Isaiah 14:12–17 describing Satan's high position as a preeminent angel prior to his fall. Satan is described here because he was the real source of power behind the king of Tyre.

Lying some twenty-three miles north of Tyre, Sidon was an important Phoenician city, strategically situated on the Mediterranean Sea. Although it was inferior to Tyre, Sidon subdued several Assyrian kings, including Tiglath-pileser I, Sennacherib, and Esarhaddon in the second millennium B.C. Sidon became more prominent than Tyre following Nebuchadnezzar's invasion of Tyre.

Before his fall, Satan was the epitome of wisdom and beauty (v. 12), when he lived in Eden. His appearance was like the brilliance and lustre of precious stones (v. 13). Before his fall, Satan had a honored position around the throne of God (v. 14). As a created angel, he was perfect before he sinned (v. 15; see Isa. 14:13–14 for a fuller description of the sin). But when Satan coveted the preeminent positon of God, he was cast out of his prominent position (v. 16). His sin—which also dominated the king of Tyre—was pride; his heart was lifted up and God cast him down (v. 17).

PROPHECY AGAINST SIDON (28:20–26)

In His judgment of Sidon, God would be glorified just as He received glory in His judgments on Paraoh (v. 22; cp. Ex. 14:4, 16–17). In His judgment, God promised to send pestilence (plague), blood (violent death), and sword (enemy invasion). Sidon would know that God was judging (v. 23). No longer would Sidon be a "prickling brier or a painful thorn" to Israel (cp. Num. 33:55; Josh. 23:13).

Israel's deliverance from this enemy merged into a picture of the future when all Israel's enemies would be subdued. In this future millennium, Israel would dwell in peace.

PROPHECY AGAINST EGYPT (29:1–32:32)

Destruction and Restoration of Egypt (29:1–16)

The Destruction (29:1–12)

The prophecy against Egypt came in the tenth year (587 B.C.) the year following Nebuchadnezzar's invasion of Jerusalem (2 Kings 25:1). The prophecy is against Pharaoh Hophra, to whom King Zedekiah of Israel had appealed for help (Jer. 37:7).

Egypt's identification is set in metaphorical language. Pharaoh Hophra was identified as "the great monster that lies in the midst of his rivers" (v. 3). Hophra is pictured as a crocodile in the Nile River (cp. Ps. 74:13; Isa. 27:1; 51:9)—an appropriate figure since the Egyptians worshiped the crocodile. As the crocodile viewed himself as god and king of the Nile, so Pharaoh Hophra saw himself as lord of the Egyptian Delta.

But the Creator is greater than the creation. God announced He would put hooks in the crocodile's jaw and bring him out of the Nile with fish clinging to his scales, throw him into the desert to die, and feed him to the animals and birds (vv. 4–5). God was promising to bring about the fall of Pharaoh Hophra (represented by the crocodile) as well as his people (represented by the fish).

The application is stated in verses 6–9. Egypt's fall was designed as an object lesson. The Egyptians would know that the Lord is God and that Hophra's demise would prove he was not God (v. 6). It was also a reminder and rebuke to Israel for the folly of trusting in Egypt instead of the Lord; Egypt was only a "staff made of reed"—too weak to sustain anyone who attempted to lean on it (v. 7). Egypt could not help Israel in its hour of crisis when the Babylonians invaded. Only the Lord could sustain them.

God would judge Egypt for their false promise to Israel and their failure to help them; He would bring a desolation of Egypt (vv. 8–12). The judgment against Egypt would cover the land from Migdol, the delta in northern Egypt, to Syene (modern Aswan), the southern border with Ethiopia.

The restoration (29:13–16)

At the conclusion of Egypt's forty year subjugation, the Egyptian nation would be restored to Pathros, in southern Egypt, where the nation had its beginnings. The forty years probably refers to Nebuchadnezzar's subjugation of Egypt when he attacked in 568 B.C. (vv. 17–21; cp. Jer. 43:10–13). Nebuchadnezzar may have taken Egyptians captive to Babylon. Later, they

The final indictment against foreign nations is also the longest. It was against Egypt, Israel's southern neighbor. The announcement of judgment against Egypt was significant for Israel since the nation looked to Egypt for help in deliverance from Babylonian oppression—in spite of Egypt's decisive defeat by Nebuchadnezzar at the battle of Carchemish in 605 in the second millennium B.C. Although the prophet Jeremiah had warned Israel against trusting in Egypt (Jer. 37:5–10), the people continued to look for help from their southern neighbor.

This prophecy was fulfilled in 570 B.C. when Pharaoh Hophra was defeated by the Greeks of Cyrene. At that time, Amasis also led an army revolt against Hophra, who was killed. Amasis then proclaimed himself king.

Perhaps without proper thought, we are prone to trust in many things instead of trusting the Lord. In an hour of crisis we may sin by *first* consulting human agencies instead of trusting the Lord. In any crisis or hour of difficulty, we should turn to the Lord *first*. He has promised to help and to respond to our cry in a crisis (Ps. 118:5; Phil. 4:6–7; 1 Pet. 5:7).

Horn frequently illustrates strength and power (1 Sam. 2:1; 2 Sam. 22:3; Pss. 89:24; 92:10; 112:9; 132:17; 148:14; Jer. 48:25; Dan. 7:8). Ultimately, it refers to the Messiah (Luke 1:69).

may have been allowed to return under Cyrus's decree (cp. Ezra 1).

Henceforth, Egypt would be a lowly kingdom—unable to lead other nations astray. This prophecy has been fulfilled in the more than two thousand years that have followed; in all its subsequent history, Egypt has never again regained its former grandeur.

Egypt's Reward to Nebuchadnezzar (29:17–21)

In April of 571 B.C., God gave Ezekiel a prophecy concerning Egypt and Babylon. For thirteen years Nebuchadnezzar had waged an arduous siege against Tyre (585–572 B.C.) during which "every head was made bald, and every shoulder was rubbed bare" from carrying heavy loads (v. 18). For his labor in attacking Tyre, Nebuchadnezzar would be rewarded by having Egypt given to him by the Lord (vv. 19–20).

At the time of the restoration of Egypt and Israel, God would make "a horn sprout for the house of Israel" (v. 21). While some think this is a reference to the Messiah, in this context it probably refers to Israel's rejuvenation and renewed strength following Babylon's conquest of Egypt.

Destruction of Egypt Described (30:1–26)

In verses 1–19 Ezekiel announced four undated oracles against Egypt and its allies, all beginning with, "Thus says the Lord God" (vv. 2, 6, 10, 13). The prophecy announced the impending destruction at the hands of Nebuchadnezzar, king of Babylon. But this prophecy also spans the ages, combining the historical judgment of Egypt with the future judgment of Egypt and the nations during the prophetic Day of the Lord in the tribulation.

Destruction of Egypt's Power (30:1–5)

This day of judgment would be a day of clouds, symbolic of God's presence in judgment at the end of the age (32:7; Dan. 7:13; Joel 2:2; Zeph. 1:15). It would surpass the judgment upon Egypt alone; it would be a judgment upon nations (v. 3; cp. Matt. 25:31–32; Rev. 19:15).

Egypt as well as its allies would be judged. The foreign nations (v. 5) represent mercenary soldiers—a mixed people identified by the term *Arabia* (Heb. *ereb*).

Devastation of the Land (30:6–9)

Egypt's allies would be unable to sustain the nation in the day of judgment; the devastation of Egypt would extend from the north (Migdol) to the south (Syene) (see discussion on 29:10). And Egypt would recognize that the Lord had spoken (v. 8). Messengers carrying the news of Egypt's devastation would create alarm and panic in Ethiopia, which would realize its own destruction was at hand (v. 9).

Devastation of the Canals (30:10–12)

Egypt's adversary and conqueror is identified: Nebuchadnezzar, king of Babylon. The ruthless king (28:7; 30:10–11; 32:12) would slay the Egyptians while the canals in the Nile Delta would be dried up (v. 12). Since the Nile was the source of Egypt's life, the land would become desolate. While God would use a human instrument in judgment, God was identified as the source of the judgment (v. 12).

Destruction of the cities of Egypt (30:13–19)

In this section Ezekiel detailed the specific cities throughout the land of Egypt that would be destroyed. Particular judgment would be aimed at the idols and images of Egypt (v. 13). Memphis, the great religious center and former

The term *Day of the Lord* may be used in several different ways: (1) It may refer to God's judgment at any point in history, such as this judgment upon Egypt. (2) It may refer to God's judgment on the gentile nations at the end of the age. (3) It may refer to God's blessing and restoration of Israel at the establishment of the millennial kingdom at the second coming of Christ. It is not unusual for a prophet to combine these concepts—and that appears to be the usage here (cp. Isa. 13:1–22; 19:1–25; Joel 1:15; 2:1–11; 3:14–16; Amos 5:18; Obad. 15; Zeph. 1:7–18).

The pagan Egyptian temples that God would destroy must have been magnificent structures. The people thought these beautiful buildings would stand forever. The Jews had a similar thought concerning the Temple in Jerusalem—but God destroyed them all (vv. 13–19; cp. Matt. 24:1–2). What was wrong? The people put their trust in a building rather than God. We may have beautiful sanctuaries in which to worship God, but we must always remember that the preeminence belongs to God alone—never to a building. God is our focus, not a building.

This is probably a reference to Pharaoh Neco's defeat by Nebuchadnezzar at the battle of Carchemish in 605 B.C. as well as Nebuchadnezzar's subsequent invasion of Egypt in 568 B.C.

capital of Egypt just ten miles south of Cairo, would suffer destruction (v. 13). Phtah ("fire-god"), the first and oldest of deities to be called "the father of the fathers of the gods," was at Memphis. Pathros in Upper (southern) Egypt; Zoan in the eastern Nile Delta (the former Hyksos capital); and Thebes, the ancient Egyptian capital in Upper Egypt and center of the worship of Amon—all of these would also suffer destruction (v. 14). And in the Nile delta, Sin (Pelusium), the strategic fortress guarding against Mediterranean invaders, would suffer God's wrath (v. 15).

His wrath would also consume On (or Heliopolis) with its sun temple and worship of the sun god as well as Pi-beseth where a cat-headed goddess was worshiped (v. 17). And for Tahpanhes, on the Suez Canal, the city where Jeremiah was taken (Jer. 43:7)— it would also be a day of gloom (v. 18). When God judged Egypt, that nation's enslaving tyranny would end (Lev. 26:13), and the people would know that the Lord had spoken (v. 19).

Dispersion of Egypt (30:20–26)
In an oracle dated in April of 587 B.C., God announced he had broken the arms of Pharaoh; the Lord removed their strength (v. 21). No longer would the Egyptians wield a sword against their enemies (v. 22). Instead, they would be scattered among the nations (v. 23). Repeatedly, God indicated He would destroy and scatter the Egyptians by using the king of Babylon (vv. 24, 25).

S N

- *Egypt, the nation to which Israel turned for*
- *help because of Babylon's oppression of*
- *Israel, would be destroyed. Israel sinned in*
- *trusting in Egypt rather than in God; now*
- *God would remove the object of Israel's false*
- *trust by destroying Egypt. The focal point of*
- *Egypt's destruction would also be the great*
- *cities with their idolatrous worship centers.*
- *God would use Nebuchadnezzar, king of*
- *Babylon, to accomplish His divine judgment*
- *of Egypt.*

Allegory of the Great Cedar (31:1–18)

In case Egypt considered itself invincible, God reminded Egypt of Assyria's grandeur, comparing the nation to a stately cedar. But God destroyed that great empire. In this allegory, God revealed that He would destroy Egypt just as he had destroyed Assyria.

The Distinction of Assyria (31:1–9)

In June of 587 B.C.,—two months following the preceding oracle—God addressed Egypt, comparing the nation to Assyria. Like the giant cedar, Assyria's domination spread over a vast area. The cedar's high branches illustrated Assyria's grandeur; providing "forest shade" suggested Assyria's widespread territory (v. 3). The waters and rivers that made Assyria grow were the Tigris and Euphrates Rivers—the water highways that brought subjugated nations, paying their tribute to Assyria (v. 4; cp. 2 Kings 15:19–20; 2 Chron. 28:19–21). The birds nesting in the branches and the animals in the fields illustrated the smaller nations subjugated by Assyria (v. 6; cp. 17:23; Dan. 4:12). Syria, Phoenicia, Israel, Judah, Ammon, Edom,

Beautiful and possessing a fragrant aroma, a cedar could attain a height of 120 feet and a girth of 30 to 40 feet. The cedar branches spread widely and quickly. The cedar is an apt picture of growth and strength (Ps. 92:12; Ezek. 17) as well as power and wealth (1 Kings 10:27).

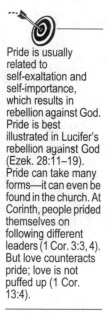

Pride is usually related to self-exaltation and self-importance, which results in rebellion against God. Pride is best illustrated in Lucifer's rebellion against God (Ezek. 28:11–19). Pride can take many forms—it can even be found in the church. At Corinth, people prided themselves on following different leaders (1 Cor. 3:3, 4). But love counteracts pride; love is not puffed up (1 Cor. 13:4).

and Moab fell under Assyria's power. The "many waters" to which the tree roots extended reflected the numerous nations under Assyria's bondage (v. 7). Assyria was an incomparable nation (v. 8) so that other nations became jealous of Assyria's might and power (v. 9).

The Downfall of Assyria (31:10–14)

Just as the towering cedars illustrated pride by their height, so Assyria was guilty of arrogance (v. 10). For this reason, God would judge Assyria, delivering the nation into the hands of a despot—the mighty Nabopolassar, king of Babylon. This was fulfilled in 612 B.C. Assyria's punishment was according to its sin (v. 11).

Like a towering tree that has been felled, with its branches cut off, so Assyria was destroyed by the Babylonians. And just as the birds forsook the fallen tree, so the nations dominated by Assyria no longer were subject to the destroyed nation (v. 12). Now the smaller nations would have the advantage—just as the birds and animals would feed on the decaying tree (v. 13). Assyria's destruction was an object lesson to other nations. They were warned not to exalt themselves or they would suffer the same judgment (v. 14).

The Descent into Sheol (31:15–18)

Just as mourners cover their heads, so the springs and rivers dried up, and the trees wilted in mourning for the demise of Assyria (v. 15). This showed that the source of Assyria's wealth was dried up (v. 15). The nations trembled in fear at Assyria's destruction and descent into Sheol, while the nations in Sheol were comforted by Assyria's demise as it shared their own fate (v. 16).

The application of the allegory is given in verse 18 in a question addressed to Egypt. To whom can Egypt liken itself? To which of the trees of Eden (i.e., the nations of the earth) can it liken itself? Is it equal to the greatest? Yet Egypt will also be judged and brought down to Sheol, where it will share the fate of pagan, uncircumcised nations—an insult to the Egyptians who practiced circumcision (v. 18).

- *Although Egypt prided itself on its glorious*
- *position, God reminded Egypt that it was no*
- *greater than Assyria, the mightiest of*
- *nations. Yet God judged Assyria, using the*
- *Babylonians as its destroyers. So Egypt itself*
- *would be judged.*

Lamentation over Pharaoh and Egypt (32:1–32)

In March of 585 B.C., eighteen months after the preceding prophecy (31:1), Ezekiel took up a lamentation concerning Pharaoh of Egypt.

Lamentation over Pharaoh (32:1–16)

Egypt had fancied itself as a lion, ferocious king of the jungle, but in fact, Egypt was no more than a crocodile thrashing about in the river, muddying the waters. This picture suggested that Egypt disturbed the peace of its neighbors (v. 2). But Egypt would be captured like a crocodile caught in a net and hauled ashore where the birds and animals would feed on it (vv. 3, 4; cp. 29:4). Pharaoh's power and empire would disintegrate. Instead of water from the Nile River enriching the land, blood of the Egyptians would flow through the land (v. 6). Like a light

Sheol may refer to the grave (Job 17:13; Ps. 16:10; Isa. 38:10) or the place where all dead people go, whether good or evil (Gen. 37:35; 42:38; 44:29, 31; Ps. 55:15; Prov. 9:18). The righteous are rescued from Sheol (Ps. 16:9–11; 49:15); unbelievers go to Sheol at death (Ps. 9:17; 31:17; 49:14; 55:15). The O.T. usage of *Sheol* emphasizes where bodies go more than souls. All people go to the grave at death; however, the O.T. has little to say about the destiny of the soul. The N.T. provides fuller understanding of these matters (Matt. 25:46; Luke 16:19–31; 23:43; 2 Cor. 5:8; Phil. 1:21).

that is extinguished, so Pharaoh's power would be snuffed out (v. 7).

Cast in the imagery of the future Day of the Lord, Pharaoh's demise depicted the future day when the Lord would judge not only Egypt but also the nations of the earth (vv. 7, 8; Isa. 13:10; 34:4; Joel 2:10, 31; 3:15; Matt. 24:29; Rev. 6:12; 8:12).

Pharaoh's demise would bring distress and horror among the people of the world (26:15–18; 27:28–32; 28:19), as they realized their own impending destruction (vv. 9, 10).

While Pharaoh's destruction is described in verses 1–10, verses 11–16 detail the agent of Pharaoh's defeat—Nebuchadnezzar, king of Babylon (v. 11). The Babylonians, "tyrants of the nations"—suggestive of their ferocity—will decimate the Egyptians (v. 12). The "pride of Egypt"—its power—would be destroyed (v. 12; cp. 30:6, 18). Then the waters would settle; the turmoil that Pharaoh had stirred up and the terror among the nations would be stilled (v. 14). Through Pharaoh's death and the deportation of the Egyptians, peace would flow smoothly like rivers of oil (v. 14).

Lamentation over Egypt (32:17–32)
Two weeks after the previous oracle (32:1), Ezekiel graphically described Egypt's descent into the nether world, a reference to the burial of the Egyptians following their defeat and destruction (v. 18). "Pit," meaning "cistern" or "dungeon," is a synonym, describing Egypt's descent into Sheol (Isa. 14:15; 38:18; Ps. 28:1). The concept of a pit revealed a state of consciousness after death (Lam. 3:53–56; Ps. 30:3; Isa. 14:15–19). Sheol (see discussion under 31:15–18) was the place where all people went at death

(Gen. 37:35; 42:38; 44:29, 31; Num. 16:30, 33; 1 Sam. 2:6; Job 26:6; Ps. 55:16). These three terms emphasized the death and descent of Egypt into the place of the dead.

Along with Egypt, other great nations and smaller nations would descend to Sheol. The great nation of Assyria, defeated by Nabopolassar, king of Babylon in 612 B.C., preceded Egypt into Sheol, where the deposed monarch was surrounded by his slain warriors (vv. 22–23).

Elam, the ones who instilled terror in others in life, were lying among the uncircumcised in Sheol (vv. 24–25).

Elam was in the east (the location of modern Iran) with Susa as its capital (Dan. 8:2). The Elamites, who were non-Semitic people, existed early in history (Gen. 10:22) and became a great people during the time of Abraham. Defeated by Ashurbanipal of the Assyrians in 640 B.C., they were absorbed into the Persian Empire.

Meshech and Tubal (see comment on 27:13) were also in Sheol in dishonor. Because of their barbarity, they did not lie with the fallen heroes (v. 27). Verse 28 is addressed to Egypt: Like the preceding nations, Egypt would also be destroyed and descend to Sheol. Edom, Israel's ancient enemy to the south, would also lie among the uncircumcised in Sheol—an insult since Edom practiced circumcision. To the north, the Sidonians (a general term for the Phoenicians) and the "princes of the north"—the people living along the Phoenician coastline would also be defeated and descend to Sheol (v. 30).

Upon arriving in Sheol, Pharaoh would be comforted when he saw all the defeated empires before his time, nevertheless, for his attrocities, Pharoah would also descend to Sheol (vv. 31–32).

In Akkadian sources, the nether world is pictured as a cheerless place, a kind of cavern deep in the earth where people go at death—a place of deprivation and hardship. But this is not the O.T. picture. Ezekiel seems to use "nether world" as a synonym for the grave. In this thought, the nether world refers to a burial cave where bodies were buried, sometimes in state and with their armor (Ronald Youngblood, "tahti," Theological Wordbook of the O.T., 2:968–969).

■ *Although Egypt had achieved greatness, like*
■ *a helpless crocodile in the river, Pharaoh*
■ *would be captured and he and his people*
■ *would descend to Sheol, the place of the*
■ *departed dead. Here Pharaoh would see*
■ *other past empires, destroyed and judged for*
■ *their barbarous deeds.*

QUESTIONS TO GUIDE YOUR STUDY

1. Against how many nations did Ezekiel announce judgment?
2. What brought God's judgment against the great city of Tyre?
3. Why would judgment be brought against Egypt?
4. Who would be God's instrument of judgment against Egypt?

PROPHECIES OF ISRAEL'S RESTORATION AND BLESSING (33:1–39:29)

The second major message of the prophet, a message of comfort for the people with the hope of future restoration and blessing in the millennial kingdom, is emphasized in these chapters.

PREDICTION OF ISRAEL'S FUTURE BLESSING (33:1–34:31)

Chapters 33–34 mark the turning point in the book. When news of Jerusalem's destruction reached Ezekiel and the exiles, Ezekiel's restriction was removed so that he spoke freely to the people (33:22; cp. 3:26, 27; 24:27; 29:21). Ezekiel warned the people of the false shepherds that led the nation astray and promised the coming of the true shepherd, the Messiah, who would shepherd His people in truth.

Designation of the Watchman (33:1–33)
His commission (33:1–9)

Ezekiel's call as a spiritual watchman of Israel is a repetition of 3:16–21. In chapter 33, his call is repeated for emphasis and as a prelude to the message of comfort to follow (chaps. 33–48; see chaps. 3 and 18 for further comments).

The spiritual application of the watchman is given in verses 7–9. As a watchman warned a city's inhabitants against the danger of an enemy invasion, so God appointed Ezekiel as a spiritual watchman of Israel to warn the wicked. If they did not turn from their wicked ways, they would die in their sins; but the prophet would not be responsible (v. 9). In Ezekiel's thought, to "live" meant to live physically in the land and

For protective purposes, it was common to build a city on a hill in ancient Israel. A watchman, who would scan the countryside to watch for possible enemy attack, was stationed on the city wall. This was a grave responsibility since the watchman's failure to warn the city's inhabitants could lead to their deaths through an unexpected attack. If the watchman saw an enemy approaching, he would blow a trumpet, warning the inhabitants to prepare to defend themselves (cp. 2 Sam. 18:24–27; 2 Kings 9:17–20; Jer. 6:1; Hos. 8:1; Amos 3:6; Hab. 2:1). If the people failed to respond to the warning blast and they died, the watchman was innocent (v. 4; 18:13). But if the watchman saw the approaching enemy and failed to warn the people, he was responsible for their deaths (v. 6).

inherit the promises of the millennial kingdom to come (cp. Ezek. 37); to "die" meant exclusion from Messiah's coming kingdom.

His Message (33:10–20)

With the news of Jerusalem's destruction and their own plight in exile in a foreign country, the people despaired, crying out in anguish over their sins which had caused this dilemma (v. 10). Confronting their despair, Ezekiel brought a message of comfort and hope (v. 11). God did not desire their death; the solution was repentance. (For "repentance," see comment under 14:1–11). The repentance involved a return in obedience to the Mosaic Law. The Israelites were bound to God under the Mosaic covenant (Exod. 19). For the Israelite, true repentance meant a return to obedience to the Mosaic Law. If a righteous man failed to repent and return, he would be judged; conversely, if a wicked man repented, his sins would not be held against him (vv. 12–16; see 3:16–21; 18:3–32 for further discussion).

When the people objected that the Lord's way was unjust (v. 17), Ezekiel reminded them of the Lord's justice in judging the people (v. 20; cp. 18:25–32).

His Freedom to Speak (33:21–33)

In January of 585 B.C., news of Jerusalem's destruction reached Ezekiel and the exiles. With this announcement, God removed the earlier restriction on Ezekiel, permitting him to move and minister freely among the people (v. 22; cp. 3:26–27).

Ezekiel addressed the poor remnant of Jews living in the land of Israel following the devastation by the Babylonians (vv. 23–29). They were still haughty, arguing that if Abraham alone could possess the land, surely they, who were many, could possess it (v. 24). They assumed they would inherit the land because of their physical descent from Abraham—but without their obedience. However, Abraham obeyed God whereas they disobeyed Him. They ate meat with blood (Lev. 17:10), being guilty of the crimes that caused Jerusalem's destruction: idolatry (v. 25; cp. 18:6, 12, 15). They also committed murder (v. 25; cp. 18:10) and adultery (v. 26) and trusted their swords instead of trusting God. God pronounced judgment on them (v. 27). They would perish and the land would become desolate (vv. 27–28)—then they would realize that God had spoken (v. 29).

Pride is a subtle thing, and it is easy for a Christian to fall into pride as well—pride in belonging to a particular church, pride in social status, pride in a business or church position. But ultimately all pride is doomed to failure because it results in merely listening to God's Word without the corresponding obedience. God blesses those who listen, then come to Him in humility and obedience (James 1:22–25).

In verses 30–33, the Lord revealed the corrupt hearts of the people. They recognized that God had spoken to Ezekiel. They came and listened to his words, but inwardly they were filled with lustful desires. They had only a fleeting interest in Ezekiel's word—as though he were a singer of love songs. They did not practice obedience. But when Ezekiel's words came true, they would realize that Ezekiel had spoken the truth.

Description of Israel's Shepherds (34:1–31)

The False Shepherds (34:1–10)

Under the metaphor of a shepherd and sheep, this chapter contrasts the false shepherds of Israel—the kings—with the true shepherd, the Messiah. The indictment against the false shepherds is announced in verses 1–6. They lavished wealth upon themselves at the expense of the people. They oppressed the people and were negligent in their responsibilities. Instead of caring for the people, they treated them harshly and scattered them (cp. 1 Kings 22:17).

The judgment of the kings is described in verses 7–10. Before announcing the judgment, Ezekiel reminded them of their sin (v. 8). Now they would "hear the word of the Lord" in judgment (vv. 7, 9). No longer would the shepherds care for the sheep—referring to the termination of the Judean kings' rule. Pharaoh Neco imprisoned Jehoahaz (2 Kings 23:33); Nebuchadnezzar took Jehoiakim, Jehoiachin, and Zedekiah captive to Babylon (2 Chron. 36:6; 2 Kings 24:12; 25:7).

The kings of Israel were called shepherds (1 Kings 22:17; Ps. 78:70–72; Isa. 44:28; 63:11; Jer. 10:21; 23:1–6; 25:34–38; Zech. 10:2–3). As the nation's shepherds, the kings were responsible for protecting and caring for the people. Through them, God's blessings flowed to the nation.

The True Shepherd (34:11–31)

In contrast to the false shepherds of Israel, the Lord Himself promised to shepherd the people (vv. 11–16). (Note the "I will" statements.) This promise was not fulfilled in the return from captivity in Babylon; they did not have the peace promised in these verses. This promise anticipated the regathering of Israel from the countries of the world at the end of the age and Messiah's protective rule over Israel in the future millennial kingdom.

Before Messiah's rule in the millennial kingdom, He will judge the individual sheep (vv. 17–22). He will judge the sheep, the goats, the fat, and the lean within Israel (vv. 17, 20). The rams and male goats likely refer to the false leaders who led the people astray. Within Israel, the righteous would be separated from the unrighteous to determine who would enter the millennial kingdom.

In contrast to the false shepherds of Israel, the Lord would set one shepherd, David, over Israel (vv. 23–24). Some believe this will be the literal, historic David resurrected and ruling over Israel in the millennium. That is possible. Probably it is better to understand "David" as a title of Messiah. It is the Lord Himself who is the Shepherd (v. 11). In that future day in the millennial kingdom, Israel will be converted; they will know God and the Messiah who will teach them (vv. 23–24).

When Messiah returned to rescue Israel, He would establish a covenant of peace with them (vv. 25–31). They would enjoy protection from harm (vv. 25, 28) as well as productive harvest because of seasonal showers (vv. 26, 27, 29; Isa. 65:21–22; 30:23; Hos. 2:22; Joel 2:23; 3:18). Foreign powers would no longer enslave them (vv. 27, 28; Zech. 14:1–11). Israel would be converted and know the Lord (36:25–27; Zech. 12:10–13:6; Rom. 11:26–27).

"David" is the dynasty from which the Messiah will come (2 Sam. 7:12–16; Ps. 89:3–4; Matt. 1:1; 9:27; 12:23; 15:22; 20:31–31). Messiah was specifically called David on other occasions (Jer. 30:9; Hos. 3:5). The term *shepherd* is also a messianic term (Isa. 49:5–9; 50:10; 52:13–53:12).

■ *The kings—the false shepherds of*
■ *Israel—burdened the people and led them*
■ *astray. But when the Messiah returned, He*
■ *would rescue His people Israel, regather*
■ *them from the nations, convert them and*
■ *bless them spiritually and materially in the*
■ *millennial kingdom.*

PREDICTION OF ISRAEL'S FUTURE RESTORATION (35:1–37:28)

These chapters prophesy the destruction of Edom, Israel's enemy, and the future conversion and establishment of Israel in the millennial kingdom.

Prophecy of Edom's Destruction (35:1–15)

Since Edom's destruction had been foretold earlier (25:12–14), the repetition in this passage suggests Edom stood as representative of the nations of the world that afflicted Israel (cp. 36:5). Edom—and the nations of the

"Obedience brings blessing" is always a truism. While it is wrong for us in the church age to look for material blessings (although that can also happen), God blesses His people when they walk in fellowship with Him (Eph. 1:3; 1 John 1:1–10).

Mount Seir (v. 1) describes the mountain range east of the desert, the Arabah, extending from the southern end of the Dead Sea southward to the Gulf of Aqaba. This is the territory inhabited by the Edomites.

world—would be judged because of their persecution of Israel.

Edom's judgment is pronounced in verses 1–4. God promised to destroy the cities of Edom and make the land a desolation. The hand of God is a figure of speech describing the strength of God—either on behalf of someone or against someone. God's hand would be stretched out in judgment against Edom.

Two reasons for God's judgment are given in verses 5–6. Because of their enduring hostility toward Israel (2 Sam. 8:13–14) and because Edom assisted Nebuchadnezzar when he destroyed Jerusalem (cp. Obad. 10–14), God would give the Edomites over to bloodshed. Because Edom did not abhor the suffering and death of the Israelites, Edom would experience death (v. 6).

The judgment is described in verses 7–9. The land of Edom would become a wasteland, no longer profiting from caravans crossing its territory. Ultimately, Edom would cease to exist—a prophecy fulfilled in A.D. 70.

Further reasons for Edom's destruction is given in verses 10–11. Edom coveted the land of Israel and Judah ("these two nations" and "these two lands"), hoping to possess them and profit from them. But Edom would be judged "according to" its hatred (v. 11). Theirs was an act of aggression against the Lord Himself since He lived there (v. 10). In judgment, God would make Himself known to Edom.

Moreover, God was listening. He heard Edom reviling Israel (v. 12) and speaking arrogantly—against the Lord Himself (v. 13)! But God would make Edom a desolate wasteland.

As Edom had rejoiced in the destruction of Israel, so others would rejoice over Edom's destruction (vv. 14–15).

■ *Edom, the archenemy of Israel and represen-*
■ *tative of the nations' hostility toward Israel,*
■ *would be judged and destroyed for her hatred*
■ *of Israel.*

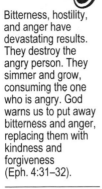

Bitterness, hostility, and anger have devastating results. They destroy the angry person. They simmer and grow, consuming the one who is angry. God warns us to put away bitterness and anger, replacing them with kindness and forgiveness (Eph. 4:31–32).

Prophecies of Israel's Restoration (36:1–37:28)

Israel's glorious conversion and repopulation of the land of Israel in the future is detailed in these chapters. The mountains, hills, valleys, and cities would again be populated—but first God would regenerate the people of Israel in a spiritual sense.

Restoration of the Land of Israel (36:1–15)

Because Israel had experienced hostility and suffering at the hands of its enemies, God addressed the "mountains of Israel"—the land and the people—with a prophecy of future blessing (v. 1). The land that had suffered devastation would again be cultivated, but judgment would be leveled against the enemies of Israel—including Edom (v. 5). Five times Ezekiel declared "therefore," emphasizing the enemies' destruction (vv. 3, 4, 5, 6, 7).

The general statement of Israel's future blessing is stated in verse 8, with an amplification in verses 9–15. These prophecies were not fulfilled in the return from Babylon in 586 B.C. At that time, Israel continued to experience hostility from their enemies. But at the second advent of Christ and the establishment of the millennial kingdom, Israel would again know peace and prosperity in their land. The reason for Israel's blessing is stated in verse 9—God would be with them. He would subjugate their enemies and cause them to prosper. The people would return to the land and multiply (v. 10). Their cities would be populated (v. 10); their cattle would multiply (v. 11) and their blessing would be unparalleled (v. 11). Moreover, it would be a permanent peace; never again would they endure persecution and suffering at the hands of enemies (vv. 14–15). The emphatic "no longer . . . any more . . any longer" indicates Israel's permanent peace in the millennial kingdom under Messiah's rule (vv. 14–15).

Restoration of the People of Israel (36:16–38)

Before describing Israel's future cleansing and conversion, the Lord reminded Israel of the reason for their captivity in Babylon and their dispersion among the nations (vv. 16–21). They had defiled the Lord's land with their idolatry (36:17, 18; cp. Lev. 18:24–28; 2 Kings 21:1–15); for this reason God poured out His judgment on them (7:8; 9:8; 14:19; 16:38; 20:8, 13, 21; 22:22; 30:15). They even profaned His name among the gentile nations (vv. 21, 22); yet the Lord had concern for His name—He refused to abandon Israel.

But God promised to vindicate His holy name which had been profaned among the nations (v. 23); He would regather the Israelites and restore them to the Promised Land (v. 24). As a testimony to the nations, the Lord would bring them back into their "own land" (v. 24), promised to them by covenant centuries earlier (Gen. 15:18–21; Deut. 30:1–10).

The condition for Israel's future restoration and blessing in the land was their spiritual conversion (vv. 25–32). God promised to sprinkle clean water on them (cp. Lev. 15:21–22; Num. 17–19), a metaphor describing their cleansing from idolatry (v. 25) but also their conversion and forgiveness (cp. Ps. 51:2–4, 7–9). Through conversion they would receive a new heart, enabling them to fulfill the most basic command (Deut. 6:5). With the new heart, their rebellion would be removed. They would also receive a new human spirit as well as the indwelling Holy Spirit (vv. 26, 27).

At Pentecost, the Holy Spirit was poured out. This was a nonrepeatable experience, making provision for Israel's spiritual blessing (Acts 2). However, Israel's appropriation of the Holy Spirit would occur at the second advent of Christ, when they repented (Zech. 12:10–14) and were regenerated and converted (Ezek. 36:25–27; 37:14; 39:29; Isa. 44:3; 59:21; Joel 2:28–29). As a result, Israel would be inwardly motivated to obey the Lord (v. 27) and walk in fellowship with Him (v. 28), repudiating their former sinful life (v. 31). Israel's blessings would overflow into the material realm in the millennium (vv. 29–30).

In concert with Israel's spiritual blessings would be their material blessings in the land (vv. 33–36). The restoration would be so thorough that the land would be likened to the Garden of Eden (v. 35). Even the gentile nations would recognize that the Lord had done this (v. 36).

There would be no holocaust, no violence against Israel in that day; but Israel would see a population explosion as the land and cities were

"Heart" does not describe the physical organ but the moral character of the person, the inner person—the seat of the will, emotions, and conscience (Brown, Drive, Briggs, Hebrew-English Lexicon, p. 525; Unger & White, Expository Dictionary of the O.T., pp. 177–178). The new heart gives the believer a new ability to love and obey God and to serve Him with a new desire and motivation.

It is impossible to love God and serve Him without spiritual conversion. The command of Christ, "You must be born again" (John 3:3), is essential to a new life. Through faith in Christ's atoning work, regeneration and conversion take place, enabling the believer to love and obey God (Matt. 22:37).

"Breath" (37:5) is the Hebrew word *ruah*, which may be translated "breath" (vv. 5, 6, 8, 9, 10), "winds" (v. 9), or "Spirit" (vv. 1, 14). The context must determine the meaning of ruah, since it has a wide range of meanings. Ultimately, it means activity and life (Job 17:1; Judg. 15:19) that comes from God to all mankind (Job 12:10; Isa. 42:5) through God's special creative act (Gen. 2:7) (J. B. Payne, "ruah," Theological Wordbook of the O.T., 2:836–837).

repopulated like flocks of sheep filling the city on a feast day (vv. 37–38).

■ *At the second advent of Christ, the Lord will*
■ *remove Israel's suffering as the people are*
■ *spiritually converted. Then God will bless*
■ *them spiritually and materially as they*
■ *repopulate the land of Israel and enjoy the*
■ *bounty of the Lord's material blessings.*

Restoration as One Nation (37:1–28)

In this vision, Ezekiel saw the restoration of Israel and Judah as one nation, reunited under Messiah's rule. This vision illustrated the promise of chapter 36.

VISION OF THE DRY BONES (37:1–14)

In a vision reminiscent of 8:3 and 11:5, 24, Ezekiel was transported to a valley filled with dry bones. The bones, depicting death, were very dry, revealing they had been dead a long time. The future appeared hopeless: "Can these bones live?" (v. 3). The bones portrayed a nation of people, hence, "Can these people—this nation—be brought to life?" God alone knew the answer (v. 3).

As Ezekiel prophesied over the bones at the Lord's instructions, he heard a rattling, and the dry bones began to come to life. They connected properly to each other; sinews, flesh, and skin covered the bones (v. 8). God breathed the breath of life into the skeletons and they came to life (vv. 9, 10; cp. Ps. 104:29, 30).

The explanation of the vision is given in verses 11–14. Specifically, the phrase "these bones are the whole house of Israel" explains the vision

(v. 11). This vision does not describe individual resurrection but the restoration of the "whole house of Israel"—Israel and Judah—to the land of Israel at the end of the age. The graves (v. 12) represented the foreign nations from which the Israelites would return to the Promised Land. But, in concert with 36:25–27, God will regenerate them, putting His Holy Spirit within them, while bringing them into the land (v. 14; 39:29; Joel 2:28; Isa. 32:15). This prophecy is not fulfilled by the Jews who live in Israel today; it will be fulfilled when believing Jews return to the land at the return of Jesus Christ (Matt. 24:30–31).

SYMBOL OF THE ONE STICK (37:15–28)

This symbolic act further developed the promise of chapter 36 and the vision of 37:1–14. Ezekiel was instructed to take two sticks, write "Judah" (representing the Southern Kingdom) on one and "Joseph" (representing the Northern Kingdom) on the other (v. 16). Then Ezekiel was to join them as one in his hand (v. 17).

This symbolic act is explained in verses 18–23, particularly verses 21–22. God promised to regather the Israelites from the foreign nations and bring them as a unified nation, as one people, back into the land. Although they had been divided as two nations since the death of Solomon (931 B.C.), at the return of Christ they would be united as one nation; moreover, they would be converted, spiritually cleansed from their idolatry (v. 23).

After Israel is reunited in the land and spiritually alive, David would be king over them (v. 24). David is a messianic title of Jesus Christ (see comment on 34:24). Because of Israel's conversion (36:25–27) and Messiah's rule over them, they will live in obedience to the Lord. The Israelites will live in the land "forever," throughout the millennium, fulfilling the promise of the unconditional Abrahamic Covenant (Gen. 12:1–3; 13:14–18; 15:12–21; 28:13–15). God's sanctuary will be among them, a reference to the millennial Temple (Ezek. 40–43). God's glory will again dwell with Israel (cp. 10:18; 11:23; 43:4).

Sometimes believers become discouraged by political and world events. How will history conclude? Will evil overtake and consume the world? God has written the last chapter of history. History will consummate with the triumphant return of Jesus Christ and His glorious reign on earth. Christian, take heart!

■ *At the return of Christ, the Jewish people will*
■ *be regathered to the land from the foreign*
■ *nations where they have been scattered. They*
■ *will come back to the land in faith, believing*
■ *in Jesus as the Messiah and living in obedi-*
■ *ence to Him throughout the millennium.*

PROPHECIES OF GOG'S JUDGMENT (38:1–39:29)

These chapters form a unit, describing God's intervention on behalf of Israel in establishing Israel in the land. A coalition of northern nations invaded Israel but were destroyed by God as they entered the land of Israel (38:17–39:8). Burial of the enemies' dead took seven months (39:12), Israel was securely established in the land (39:25–29), and God's glory was manifested to the nations (39:21–24).

Gog's Invasion (38:1–16)

Ezekiel pictured a massive invasion against Israel by a coalition of nations. When would the invasion take place? The context indicates the *general* time period must be future—at the end of the age. Ezekiel had described Israel's future restoration (34:11–31; 36:1–37:28), the nations that had persecuted Israel were to be judged (35:1–15; 36:7; 38:1–39:29), and the millen-

nial blessings would follow (40:1–48:35). Ezekiel also identified the time as "in the latter
years" (38:8) and "in the last days" (38:16).

Within the framework of the future, several
interpretations have been suggested:

(1) The invasion would take place before the
rapture of the church. Problem: Ezekiel pictured Israel living in peace in the land whereas
Luke 21:24 indicates Israel would not enjoy
peace during the times of the Gentiles. Israel
would not live in peace until the world ruler
signed the peace agreement with Israel (Dan.
9:27) or the Messiah returned.

(2) The invasion would take place at the end of
the tribulation. Problem: There is considerable
dissimilarity between Ezekiel 38 and Revelation
19 (and Zech. 14:1–4).

(3) The invasion would take place at the beginning of the millennium. Problem: Who will lead
the army if the beast and false prophet have
been judged and cast into the lake of fire and
Satan is bound in the pit (Rev. 19:20; 20:1–3)?
Unbelievers will have been judged and their
weapons destroyed (Mic. 4:1–4).

(4) The invasion would take place at the end of
the millennium. Problem: There are numerous
discrepancies between Ezekiel 38 and Revelation 20. Further, why bury the dead if the resur
rection of the unsaved takes place at the end of
the millennium (Rev. 20:11–15)?

(5) The invasion would take place just prior to
the middle of the tribulation. This seems best to
fit the context and related passages. Israel is portrayed as living at peace in the land (38:8, 11)
because of a guarantee of peace by the Antichrist
(Dan. 9:27).

The names *Rosh,
Meshech*, and *Tubal*
represent historic
place names in
existence in Ezekiel's
day.

91

The names *Gog, Rosh, Meshech,* and *Tubal* were historic names that should be understood *representatively* or *eschatologically.* Ezekiel prophesied concerning a future invasion against Israel, but used names of nations during his day because the future invaders would be from the same geographical places.

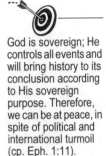

God is sovereign; He controls all events and will bring history to its conclusion according to His sovereign purpose. Therefore, we can be at peace, in spite of political and international turmoil (cp. Eph. 1:11).

While they were responsible for their actions, the invaders are seen as supernaturally drawn from their homelands, like wild beasts (v. 4) to invade the land of Israel. Although Ezekiel described the invasion as with "horses and horsemen . . . wielding swords" (v. 4), it is not necessary to suggest the final battle will be fought with horses. How would Ezekiel describe future warfare? Since he had no terminology for modern warfare, he would use the terminology of his time—horses and swords. These enemies come from the "remote parts of the north" (vv. 6, 15), modern Turkey and southern Russia—the nations surrounding the Black and Caspian Seas.

Gog's Destruction (38:17–39:20)

Their Destruction (38:17–39:8)

As the invaders entered the land of Israel God would cause a gigantic earthquake to occur that would cause all of life—fish, birds, animals, insects, and people to quake at the judgment of God (v. 20). Gog's survivors would panic and destroy one another (v. 21). And as in the days of Sodom and Gomorrah, God would rain fire and brimstone in judgment on Israel's enemies (v. 22; cp. Gen. 19:24). God would be magnified in judgment. Since God is holy, sin must be judged (v. 23).

A description of the invader's judgment and destruction is repeated for emphasis in 39:1–8.

God would destroy Gog on the mountains of Israel (vv. 2, 4). The repeated use of *I* emphasizes that God is the one who will destroy the invaders (vv. 2, 3, 4, 5, 6, 7). The invaders' weapons would be destroyed (v. 3), and the mighty army would become food for predators (v. 4). Not only would the invaders be destroyed, but the land of their origins—Magog—would also be destroyed (v. 6). God's name would be vindicated; blasphemy against God would be terminated (v. 7).

In our contemporary world, we probably do not have a proper respect for God's holiness. The problem may be that we don't take sin seriously. The two go together. If we revere God in His holiness, we will have a hatred for sin. If we take sin lightly, we will not fear and revere God.

Their Burial (39:9–20)

The plunderers would themselves be plundered as their weapons would be used for fuel for seven years, so massive was the military supply of the invaders (vv. 9, 10). "Weapons" (Heb. *nesheq*) may be translated "equipment," suggesting combustible materials.

Gog and his hordes would be buried in "the Valley of Hamon-Gog," a dead-end valley east of the Dead Sea (v. 11). They coveted Israel—they got a permanent place in Israel! So massive would the destruction be that it would take seven months to bury the dead (v. 12). People would scour the land, looking for the dead to be buried in the Valley of Hamon-Gog in order to cleanse the land from defilement (vv. 13–16; Num. 35:33–34; 5:2; 9:6–7).

Ezekiel 39:4 is developed in 39:17–20, with language reminiscent of Revelation 19:17–18. The destruction and plunder of the invaders is described. In a reversal of roles, animals would feed on the invaders as the invaders became sacrifices eaten by the animals.

God's Glory (39:21–29)

In judging Israel's enemies, God would be exalted, revealing His glory and holiness to the nations (v. 21). Israel would be converted, knowing the Lord (v. 22), and the gentile nations would recognize the holiness of God, that God sent Israel into exile because of their sin (v. 23). But in that day, God would restore Israel's fortunes by regathering them from the nations of the world, delivering them from the tribulation, and bringing them back into the land for their blessing in the millennial kingdom (v. 27). Ezekiel pictured the end of the tribulation which concluded with Israel's repentance (Zech. 12:10–14; Matt. 24:30) and appropriation of the Holy Spirit's blessing in the millennium (39:29; Isa. 44:3; Joel 2:28–29).

The holiness of God is a dominant theme of Scripture (Lev. 11:44; 1 Pet. 1:16). Israelites in the O.T. and church age believers in the N.T. are called to holiness—a life "set apart" for God and "set apart" from sin. God is a holy God—entirely separated from sin—and He commands His people to be holy.

■ *Near the middle of the tribulation, a Muslim*
■ *coalition will invade Israel. God will supernat-*
■ *urally destroy them on the mountains of Israel,*
■ *and they will be buried east of the Dead Sea.*
■ *Israel will repent, and the nations of the world*
■ *will recognize the holiness of God in judging*
■ *sin at the beginning of the millennium.*

QUESTIONS TO GUIDE YOUR STUDY

1. Following the destruction of Jerusalem, what was Ezekiel's message to Israel in exile?

2. How do false and true shepherd's differ?

3. What is the meaning of the vision of dry bones?

4. What are some of the interpretations of the massive invasion of Israel by a coalition of nations in the last days? Which interpretation do you take?

PROPHECIES OF WORSHIP IN THE MILLENNIAL KINGDOM (40:1–48:35)

Israel's spiritual conversion and physical restoration to the land are described in chapters 33–39; chapters 40–48 deal with Israel's worship during the millennium that follows its restoration to the land.

THE TEMPLE REESTABLISHED (40:1–43:27)

Ezekiel provides a detailed description of a temple—but what temple did he describe? Several interpretations have been suggested:

(1) It is Solomon's Temple, given to encourage the people. Problem: The description and dimensions do not fit Solomon's Temple.

(2) It is Zerubbabel's Temple, built when the Jews returned from Babylon. Problem: The details do not correspond; further, the glory of God returns to Ezekiel's temple (43:4) but does not return to Zerubbabel's Temple.

(3) It refers to the church. Problem: This is allegorical interpretation which forces a hidden or mystical meaning on the ordinary meaning of words. That interpretation, which abandons proper principles of interpretation, specifically, the literal-grammatical-historical method of interpretation, is wrong.

(4) It is the millennial temple. This view best fits the context as well as the meaning of the words themselves. After Israel is converted and restored to the land, a temple will be built for

"Shekinah"

Transliteration of Hebrew word not found in the Bible but used in many Jewish writings to speak of God's presence. The term means "that which dwells," and is implied throughout the Bible whenever it refers to God's nearness either in a person, object, or His glory.

Israel's worship of a holy God during the millennium.

What is the purpose of this millennial temple? (1) It demonstrates God's holiness. His holiness demanded judgment of a sinful nation, but the Lord will manifest His glory among the repentant people. (2) It is a dwelling place for God's presence among His people (43:7). It is a reminder that although Israel had been chastised as a disobedient people, they are again restored, and God visibly—in the shekinah glory—dwells with them. (3) It is the center for divine government. During the millennium, God will rule over His people with Jerusalem as the universal center of His rule (43:7; Isa. 2:2; 66:20).

THE TEMPLE GATES

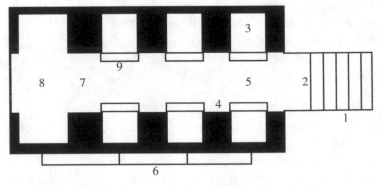

1. Seven steps (vv. 6,22,26)
2. Porch (outer, v. 8)
3. Guard chambers (vv. 7,10,12)
4. Chamber walls (v. 7)
5. Threshold (outer, vv. 6,11)
6. Chamber windows (v. 16)
7. Threshold (inner, v. 7)
8. Porch (inner, vv. 6,11)
9. Chamber door walls (v. 12)

N

- *Following Israel's spiritual conversion and*
- *restoration to the land at the end of the trib-*
- *ulation period, Jesus Christ will return to*
- *rule in the millennial kingdom. Ezekiel was*
- *given a vision of the Temple that would be*
- *constructed for worship in the millennial*
- *kingdom. The glory of God will return to fill*
- *the Temple as a sign of fellowship with His*
- *regenerated people, Israel.*

Only as we have a right understanding of God do we have a right understanding of ourselves. When we recognize God's holiness, we also recognize our sinfulness (cp. Isa. 6:1–5).

THE WORSHIP REORGANIZED (44:1–46:24)

Considerable discussion has been evoked by the institution of sacrificial offerings in Ezekiel's vision. What is the meaning of these animal sacrifices? Is this a reversion to the Old Testament Levitical system? Several things should be noted:

(1) These sacrifices are not propitiatory. Animal sacrifices could never take away sins (Heb. 10:4).

(2) These sacrifices are memorial. They are a reminder of the completed atoning work of Jesus Christ. Just as believers in the church age celebrate the Lord's Supper by looking back to Calvary, so millennial worshipers will offer sacrifices as a memorial looking back to the completed work at Calvary.

Believers in the present church age enjoy a great privilege in God's indwelling ministry. The believer's body is a temple—"Holy of Holies" (Gk. *naos*)—of the Holy Spirit (1 Cor. 6:19). Christ also indwells believers (Col. 1:27). Even the Father indwells believers (John 14:23; note plural "we"). Yea, the triune God indwells believers—a foreshadowing of millennial blessings!

(3) These sacrifices are not a reinstitution of the Levitical system. Although there are similarities with the Levitical system, there are also differences. The Temple does not have the same dimensions; also absent is the ark of the covenant, the tables of the Law, Aaron's rod, the mercy seat, the high priest, the veil, the showbread, the lampstand, and the feasts of Pentecost

and Atonement. In view of these differences, these sacrifices cannot be a reinstitution of the Levitical system.

■ *In the millennial Temple, the descendants of*
■ *Zadok will minister as priests, offering*
■ *memorial sacrifices, commemorating the*
■ *atonement of Christ. These sacrifices are not*
■ *propitiatory and are different from the sacri-*
■ *fices under the Mosaic Law.*

Millennial worship does not constitute a reinstitution of the Mosaic Law. The death of Christ did away with the Law (Rom. 7:4, 6; 10:4; Gal. 3:13, 24, 25) so that believers are under grace (Rom. 6:14). Christ set us free from the Law (Gal. 3:22).

THE LAND REDISTRIBUTED (47:1–48:35)

Historical Background

Israel was promised the land under the Abrahamic Covenant (Gen. 12:1–3; 15:12–21). The Abrahamic covenant was unconditional—its fulfillment was based on God's promise alone. The Palestinian covenant (Deut. 30:1–10) reaffirmed the promise of Israel's unconditional future restoration. Chapter 47 details the divisions and geographical changes in the land.

River from the Temple (47:1–12)

Although there are similarities between this event and Revelation 22, they are distinct. Revelation 22 refers to the eternal state; Ezekiel 47 refers to the millennium. At the entrance of the Temple, Ezekiel saw a river coming from beneath the temple threshold, flowing eastward (v. 1). The river expanded as it flowed toward the Dead Sea, first reaching the prophet's ankles, then his knees and waist, and finally it was deep enough to swim in (vv. 2–5). The river brought healing wherever it flowed (vv. 7–9), similar to the leaves of Revelation 22:2.

Boundaries of the land (47:13–23)

Regenerated and restored Israel will inherit the land in the millennium. It will be divided equally among the tribes, with Joseph receiving a double portion through his sons, Ephraim and Manasseh.

Divisions of the Land (48:1–29)

Chapter 48 describes the division of the land among the tribes in the millennial kingdom. Israel will inherit the land promised them millennia ago (Gen. 15:18–21; Deut. 30:1–10).

Gates of the City (48:30–34)

The millennial city will have twelve gates, three on each side; each gate being named after a tribe of Israel. The gates on the north side of the city—closest to the Temple—will be named after Reuben (the firstborn), Judah (the kingly/messianic tribe), and Levi (the priestly tribe) (v. 31).

Designation of the City (48:35)

The circumference of the city will be 18,000 cubits—nearly six miles. The name of the city will be "Yahweh-Shammah," meaning "The Lord Is There," emphasizing the Lord's preeminence and presence in millennial Jerusalem.

- *In the millennium, Israel will be restored to*
- *the land, exemplified by the healing river*
- *that flows from God's throne. The twelve*
- *tribes will receive equal portions of land in*
- *the millennium, the Temple and Jerusalem*
- *being central in the land. Most significant of*
- *all, the Lord will be present with His con-*
- *verted people to bless them.*

Suffering, heartache, despondency, sickness—these are things most of us can understand—we have experienced them. But the Bible provides a great word of comfort: There is a future day coming when every tear will be wiped away; sorrow will cease, suffering and heartache will no longer exist (Ezek. 47:9, 12; Rev. 21:4; 22:1–3).

God writes the last chapter of history. There is much in society to discourage people, but the believer can rejoice because history will culminate with Christ's return, judgment of sin, rescue of God's people, and the establishment of Christ's righteous reign in the millennial kingdom. Look up suffering Christian! Rejoice discouraged believer! Jesus Christ is coming again, and He will institute righteousness, comfort every believer, and wipe away every tear. Joy, peace, comfort, and gladness will belong to all believers—for eternity!

QUESTIONS TO GUIDE YOUR STUDY

1. What are four ways the reestablished Temple has been interpreted?
2. Under which Covenant was Israel given its land?
3. Which Covenant promises the restoration of Israel?
4. What is the effect of the river that Ezekiel saw flowing from the Temple?

BIBLIOGRAPHY

Alexander, Ralph. *Ezekiel*. Chicago: Moody, 1976.

Cooper, Lamar Eugene. *Ezekiel: The New American Commentary*. Nashville: Broadman & Holman, 1994.

Dyer, Charles H. "Ezekiel" in *The Bible Knowledge Commentary: Old Testament*. Wheaton, Ill.: Victor, 1985.

Enns, Paul P. *Ezekiel: Bible Study Commentary*. Grand Rapids: Zondervan, 1986.

Feinberg, Charles L. *The Prophecy of Ezekiel*. Chicago: Moody, 1969.

Gaebelein, Arno C. *The Prophet Ezekiel*. Neptune, N.J.: Loizeaux, 1972.

Keil, C. F. *Biblical Commentary on the Prophecies of Ezekiel*. 2 vols. Grand Rapids: Eerdmans, 1968 reprint.

Pearson, Anton T. "Ezekiel" in *The Wycliffe Bible Commenatry*. Chicago: Moody, 1962.

Tatford, Frederick A. *Dead Bones Live: An Exposition of the Prophecy of Ezekiel*. East Sussex: Prophetic Witness, 1977.

Taylor, John B. "Ezekiel" in *The Tyndale Old Testament Commentaries*. Downers Grove, Ill: IVP, 1969.

SHEPHERD'S NOTES

_____

_____

_____

_____

_____

_____

_____

_____

_____

_____

_____

_____

_____

_____

_____

_____

_____

_____

_____

_____

_____

_____